'The Gift' in Nietzsche's Zarathustra

'The Gift' in Nietzsche's Zarathustra

Affirmative Love and Friendship

Emilio Carlo Corriero

Translated by Vanessa di Stefano

BLOOMSBURY ACADEMIC
LONDON • NEW YORK • OXFORD • NEW DELHI • SYDNEY

BLOOMSBURY ACADEMIC
Bloomsbury Publishing Plc
50 Bedford Square, London, WC1B 3DP, UK
1385 Broadway, New York, NY 10018, USA
29 Earlsfort Terrace, Dublin 2, Ireland

BLOOMSBURY, BLOOMSBURY ACADEMIC and the Diana logo are trademarks of
Bloomsbury Publishing Plc

First published in Great Britain 2021
This paperback edition published 2023

Cover design: Charlotte Daniels
Cover image © Baivector / Shutterstock

A catalogue record for this book is available from the British Library.

Library of Congress Cataloging-in-Publication Data

Names: Corriero, Emilio Carlo, 1978- author.
Title: 'The gift' in Nietzsche's Zarathustra: affirmative love and friendship /
Emilio Corriero; translated by Vanessa di Stefano.
Other titles: Il Dono di Zarathustra. English
Description: London; New York, NY, USA: Bloomsbury Academic, 2021. |
Includes bibliographical references and index. |
Identifiers: LCCN 2021004508 (print) | LCCN 2021004509 (ebook) | ISBN 9781350212268
(hardback) | ISBN 9781350212275 (ebook) | ISBN 9781350212282 (epub)
Subjects: LCSH: Nietzsche, Friedrich Wilhelm, 1844–1900. Also sprach Zarathustra. | Gifts.
Classification: LCC B3313.A44 C6713 2021 (print) | LCC B3313.A44 (ebook) |
DDC 193–dc23
LC record available at https://lccn.loc.gov/2021004508
LC ebook record available at https://lccn.loc.gov/2021004509

ISBN: HB: 978-1-3502-1226-8
PB: 978-1-3502-1229-9
ePDF: 978-1-3502-1227-5
eBook: 978-1-3502-1228-2

Typeset by Deanta Global Publishing Services, Chonnai, India

To find out more about our authors and books visit www.bloomsbury.com and
sign up for our newsletters.

Contents

Introduction

Yes, as everyone knows,

meditation and water are wedded forever.

H. Melville, *Moby-Dick*[1]

The direct continuity Nietzsche's work paradoxically has with Christianity, his great enemy, has often been highlighted by contrasting the figure of Jesus that Nietzsche saves in the pages of *The Antichrist* with the theological construction used by Paul, or even more significantly, by substantiating the definition of 'fifth Gospel' that the philosopher himself reserves for his troubled masterpiece, *Thus Spoke Zarathustra*. However, in my view there has been little emphasis on the concept of the 'gift' and the complex and articulated dynamics that Nietzsche presents as the guiding thread of his book.[2] This is both a literary and a philosophical ploy, as crucial to understanding *Zarathustra* – but also by extension the entire last phase of Nietzsche's thought – as for the aforementioned continuity that this thought has with Christianity. This can be understood in particular if one reads Zarathustra's gift together with the renewed love at the heart of the 'fifth Gospel', as its expression and dynamics. As said, more than a concept, one should in fact speak of dynamics, that is the 'dynamics of giving' that explicitly involve the ethical level (just think of the obvious reference to the speech entitled 'On the Bestowing Virtue'), but which primarily concerns the ontological concept of the later Nietzsche. The 'ethical' reflection, if anything, comes from the latter as a consequence of the nihilistic diagnosis of the present and the tension to overcome it.

The theme of the gift is absolutely central to *Zarathustra* and, accompanying the reader throughout the entire work, from the Prologue to the fourth part added in 1885, it is the key to understanding the will to power and the possible resolution of the chaotic conflicts and problems within its dynamics. In as much as they are grafted onto the relationship between will and love, that is, onto the link fundamental to Nietzsche's reflection (but I would say to Christianity in general from Augustine onwards),[3] the gift and its associated dynamics reveal that 'impossible law' that restores *meaning* to the world in the age of 'the death of God'. The new love that replaces compassionate love is in fact the will to power oriented towards the *Übermensch* (Over-man): a will that is capable of re-giving meaning to the world, and that shows itself as a 'will to create' in that it imposes the path to overcoming upon the chaotic character of the becoming. Outside of this 'guidance', the will to power remains a permanent expression of the Chaos of eternity and responds exclusively to the preservation and continuous strengthening of the acquired positions.[4]

However, as well as enabling us to grasp the scope of the revolutionary action that Nietzsche intends to carry out in the wake of the Gospel message by rethinking love as the engine and end of will, the function of the gift is fundamental to understanding multiple aspects of the *pars construens* of Nietzsche's philosophy. In particular, through the dynamic of giving introduced by Nietzsche in *Zarathustra* it is possible to understand the meaning of the 'transvaluation of all values', as well as the axiological conception that is the basis of his reflections on passive and active nihilism.

The gift also describes the genesis and role of knowledge for Nietzsche. Zarathustra's gift is in fact a gift of wisdom (*Weisheit*) – a good that must be given, shared, so that the appropriate consequences can come from it. A gift that transforms the receiver from within. Like all gifts, it can be accepted or rejected, but it is precisely because it is a gift that it always 'scandalizes', that is, it puts the donee before an alternative whose outcome is not in the least immaterial.

However, around the figure of the gift it is also possible to reconstruct the Nietzschean concept of community, interpersonal relations, and the definition of their relationship. Fellow travellers, friends, companions, guests, simple listeners, all emerge from *Zarathustra* in their role precisely in relation to the act of receiving and giving. The phases that at first seem simply functional to the narrative take on a different and more complex meaning in *Zarathustra* if read in the light of the dynamics of giving that Nietzsche introduces as a tool for revealing the developments and processes to be corrected and overcome, and as a promoter of relational models that are effective and functional to the realization of the infinite aspiration to the *Over-man*.

More generally, it can be said that within the 'fields of meaning' in *Zarathustra*, the metaphor of giving takes on the function of connecting the key concepts that guide Nietzsche's affirmative philosophy. The 'death of God', the 'will to power' and the tension to the *Übermensch*, but also what is increasingly problematic to integrate into Nietzsche's project, namely the 'doctrine of the eternal recurrence of the same' (which can only be understood within an organic concept of time and therefore according to the overall ontological concept), all find an articulation – albeit still enigmatic and yet to be unravelled – in the gift.

This is a concept that leads to the *Chaos des Alls* (Chaos of All) as a general character of the world and therefore to a continuous becoming from which comes the possibility of the happening of the forms of being that we experience in their 'actuality'. A *Gegebenheit* (giveness) that finds an echo, of course, in our own throwness (*Geworfenheit*), in the sacredness of an unfathomed provenance that we can investigate precisely in the form of a continuous devotion to/giving of this eternal and inexhaustible becoming in the multiple forms of being.

The crucial links that Nietzsche leaves seemingly abandoned to themselves – if anything, linked together by solutions that are always problematic and revisable – therefore find composition and solution in the articulated dynamic of giving, but above all through the understanding of the particular character of 'Zarathustra's gift' described by Nietzsche.

Without any pretension to completeness with respect to the interpretation of *Thus Spoke Zarathustra* as a whole – for it would be an enterprise of a completely different kind[5] – the course I propose here clarifies some crucial conceptual knots in Nietzsche's work and thought, but at the same time opens a broader perspective yet to be explored.

Oneglia, September 2019

The dynamics of giving

Timeo Danaos et dona ferentes.

Virgil, Aeneid, II, 49

Give to take

Every gift awaits a repayment. Both Marcel Mauss[1] in his fundamental essay *The Gift* and Emile Benveniste in his important and equally fundamental etymological research[2] highlighted it very well. In the 'giving' that accompanies a 'gift' there is always a 'taking', a future 'compensation', for the gift given. Never is the giving free from the intention to take, and it is for this reason that the gift arouses that fear of obligation that always 'scandalizes' the donee: it exhorts them to accept and therefore to the escalation that follows, or it pushes them to reject that future obligation and therefore to deny the relationship offered, or reasserted, by the donor. In every giving there is always an inherent wanting to take – it is significant that, like in all Indo-European languages, the root of the verb 'to take' and of the verb 'to give' is the same: *do-*.[3]

The gift implies a 'duty', a *debitum* for the person who receives it, just as it does for they who place themselves in the position of rejecting the gift itself; but what force contained in the gift makes the donee feel obliged to respond, whether it be a refusal to reciprocate or an adherence to the 'exchange'? The 'value' of the gift that involves and requires an adequate response is not so much in the thing itself that is donated, but in the essence of the donor. Referring in particular to the Maori culture, Marcel Mauss maintains that in the objects given there is a 'soul' that binds them to the donor.[4] The donated thing preserves within itself the *hau,* or vital essence, of the donor and it is this force inherent in it that makes it return to the origin from which it came. Mauss extends this reading to universal law, that is to the innate structure present in every human being. This conclusion was criticized by Lévi-Strauss, for example, who saw it as a scientifically unsustainable extension,[5] probably due to his desire to leave areas of shadow that are unexplainable or are ascribable to an aura of mystery and magic to which Mauss was particularly susceptible. Beyond the criticism made by Lévi-Strauss and the different solutions proposed,[6] the highlighting of a sort of force or 'spirit of the gift' that activates a given dynamics cannot in any way be set aside, since therein lies the essence of the gift itself. In the dynamics of giving, one cannot but highlight a certain 'force' inherent in the gift that binds it to the donor and to the relationship within which the dynamics takes place. It is therefore in the relationship, or rather in the process that is the relationship itself, that the 'force' that Mauss evokes in reference to Maori culture must be sought.

Through the gift I want to affirm *my* worth, not the value of the gift, and – what is more – I want that 'recognition' that comes through the acceptance of the gift, because this acceptance confirms my worth in the wider sphere of social networks within which the relationship underlying the gift in question is inserted.

The donated thing is never inert. Always in some way 'animated', often individualized by the donor, and in any case 'intentional' on the part of the relationship that it aims to establish or into which it is inserted, it tends to return to the home of origin, producing an equivalence that replaces it or a surplus that keeps the donor-exchange alive and with it the underlying relationship. Certainly the 'intrinsic' value of the donated thing has its own importance – one generally gives something to which one can attribute some value regardless of the donor – but this 'value' is only the necessary packaging of an underlying and substantial *value*, constituted by the essence of the donor and the donor–donee relationship that one is going to establish or confirm. In short, we can say that the value of the donated thing depends on several variants: the donor and the donee for whom the gift is intended, the relationship between the two, the occasion and the place where the gift takes shape, the qualities of the donated thing, and so on. All aspects that must be considered together and that together determine the value of the donated object, though inevitably in a transitory way given the determination of a 'value' is always the provisional result of a continuous process.

In order to phenomenologically isolate the essential components of the act of giving, we need a donor, donee and the donated thing. It is evident that the circumstances in which a gift is made – the occasion (in an unexpected way or on a particular occasion?), the manner in which it is given (randomly or according to a precise ritual?) – are all fundamental components for the definition of the dynamics of 'giving', but what is predominant in the 'gift' is always the relationship between the giver and the one for whom the gift is intended. It is as if the giver infuses the donated thing with part of their essence, their authority, in short, part of their own *value* while waiting for the desired 'recognition'[7] of that value from the encounter with the donee and from the craved acceptance of the gift, which can also take place in different ways. It is only in the relationship that the value of the donor emerges, according to nuances of different levels that derive from the relationship itself: from the acceptance of the gift and the response that the donee chooses (when they can choose) to show therefore comes the 'valorization' of the gift, that is, of the object donated, but above all the 'recognition' of the *value* of the donor.

It is on the basis of the correspondence between donor and donee that the donated thing takes on value, and therefore that 'magic force' which gives it *intention* and redirects it to the origin from which it comes. Gifts can be of different kinds – sacrificial, commercial, ritual – and can be made in the most varied of circumstances; what is constant is the incontrovertible fact that the 'value' of the gift, its most intimate essence, that is, the force that animates it, depends unequivocally on the relationship between donor and donee. Whether the gift is inserted into a pre-existing relationship or whether the gift contributes to establishing the beginning of a form of relationship, its 'value' will always depend – both in the process of offering and possible acceptance, and in the exchange and future memory of that original donation – on the relationship between the parties involved. Confirming the transient nature of the value assigned to the gift is the relationship, which is as dynamic and susceptible to variation as it can be. Relationships, in fact, are constantly changing, since the subjects involved are constantly changing, with variations taking place both outside and inside the relationship itself.[8] It may happen that the gift has a role in these mutations, but equally often the gift may play a simply passive role with respect to these changes, and its 'value' or 'disvalue' depends on surroundings that are completely separate from the donation. A relationship that becomes strained or even breaks necessarily reflects on objects that may have previously helped to strengthen the relationship that now shows its fragility; and that object, at one time invaluable and irreplaceable, falls into indifference, taking its place in the extensive flotsam that surround us, or perhaps the mere sight of it, once welcome and rewarding, is now hateful and unbearable.[9]

One cannot separate the gift from the giver and the act that accompanies it. By responding to the gift and in any case in the act of reciprocating, one remains closely bound to the essence of the donor infused in the donated object: gift and response, whether positive or negative, are inextricably bound to the essence of the giver. The same object offered as a gift by different subjects inevitably requires different responses, not necessarily in the content of the object, perhaps only in the nuances of the 'response', in its modalities, in its timing, and this is further evidence of the fact that the value to be recognized is not in the donated object, but rather in the donor themselves and in the relationship they have with the beneficiary. Donation is an act that in itself can set aside the instrument (gift) it uses; or rather, the instrument can become decisive when with it one does not simply want to affirm one's own 'value' (that of the donor), but rather to signal a possible variation that has occurred in the relationship or for some reason to signal the disvalue of the other to whom one gives. This happens when, for example, an act of donation that is repeated cyclically in the same almost ritualistic manner, using the same 'gift' instrument (or 'gifts' that are similar) with a certain intrinsic value, suddenly changes due to the relational dynamics into which it is inserted, and it is signalled by the use of an instrument-gift with a clearly different intrinsic value.

There are evidently many variations that can be found in the description of the act of giving and here, for the purposes of this discourse, there is little point in getting lost in descriptions of the casuistry; it is enough to underline once again how through the gift one often performs an action aimed at affirming one's 'value' by demanding its 'recognition'; the gift is first of all the affirmation of the value of the donor, and it is nourished directly by the 'will to power' of the donor: this is the force that 'scandalizes' the donee, placing them before the *impasse* of having to 'respond' in some way, and since they are not given the possibility of indifference, this, too, would be a response that has repercussions on the relationship that the gift holds together.

In this form, the gift is in itself 'violent', precisely because it is simply an affirmation of power: to give means to place oneself immediately on a level of conflict and to accept the gift means to recognize the conflict itself and to try to resolve it. Rejecting a gift, on the other hand, in no way shields one from conflict, since it means either declaring one's inability to reciprocate, or – even worse, as far as the conflict is concerned – not recognizing the value of the giver. In front of the gift, the answer may mean subordinating oneself to the donor, accepting the subordination that the gift tends to reassert, or to resolutely reject the affirmation of power inherent in the donation. Already in accepting the gift, the donee begins to reciprocate it, recognizing the value of the donated thing but above all the value of the donor. The conflict inherent in the gift apparently resolves itself in the forms of this acceptance and the donee also receives the appropriate 'recognition' of their *status* in the relationship with the donor, thus avoiding open conflict. However, this *status* must be preserved in the process of donation, which is rarely completed in a single act.

Precisely because the gift owes its value to the relationship, it is always necessary to consider the persons involved in the dynamics of giving and the relationship they have with each other.

In an example that recurs quite frequently, the donee can be chosen from a peer group in order to restore unity and parity among the contracting parties; in this way the gift triggers a customary dynamics in which there is an *escalation* in the value of the object to be donated (which here is significant precisely because of the always presumed parity between the parties involved), aimed at establishing a balance of forces with clear hierarchies, but that needs to be continuously reaffirmed. In the group of peers, the person who reciprocates the gift is inclined to offer a more valuable gift than that received, both to honour the donor and to avoid the risk of subordinating themselves to the donor by losing their 'dignity' as peers. This type of gift becomes so customary that it tightens and strengthens the pact, always feeding on the underground conflict held back by the process of giving and continuous mutual recognition of the positions acquired.

When the gift is made from a level of obvious inferiority, it has no task other than to honour the power of the donee, recognize it and reaffirm it. In this case the gift is nourished by the essence of the donee, recognized and affirmed by the donor, and does not require a reward since it is already inserted into a compensation plan: that is, the donor is obliged to donate according to the value of the donee, which he cannot fail to recognize. And even if the gifts offered could never bridge the gap between the donor and donee, the dynamics of donation is entrusted with the task of giving 'dignity' to the state of subordination into which the donor necessarily enters, without any way out, to enhance the position of the donor through the relationship that, in this way, is maintained with the donee and his recognized and inalienable power.

On the other hand, if it is the donor who is in the position of obvious superiority and the donee is unable to reciprocate adequately, the gift becomes a mere and absolute (re)affirmation of power that can humiliate the donee himself, that is to say it can take on the aspect of charity – in this case the dignity of the donee is saved, at least apparently, by the charitable context of the giving.

In the picture just described there seems to be no place for a gift freed from violent dynamics, yet there are forms of gift that do not respond completely to this description. However, it is not a matter of classically distinguishing, using Seneca, between gift as *beneficium* and gift as *munus*; in fact we can immediately see how such a distinction retains all the problems described in the preceding paragraphs. It is rather a question of verifying the possibility of a gift that is free from the relational dynamics that we have tried to highlight.

Let us think, for example, of the gifts that are inserted into relationships of total otherness between the subjects involved, as happens in the case of gifts offered by men to the gods. At first it seems that this form of donation can easily be included in the already mentioned case that sees the donee in a state of superiority with respect to the donor; however, on further examination, it seems obvious that here the donee, even before being in a state of superiority, is first of all in a state of total 'otherness' with respect to the donor. Between the two subjects of the particular 'relationship' there is not a simple diversity in terms of hierarchy and rank, but rather a fundamental, we could say ontological, difference by virtue of which the gift loses its effectiveness; it is in no way binding even with regard to the preservation of the 'dignity' of the giver, since the possible response of the donee depends exclusively on the free and gratuitous will of the gods. The gift offered to the gods is always inadequate, and its possible value derives solely from absolute otherness, from the divine essence, and no longer from the mediation between donor and donee. One offers to the gods in order to quiet their anger or to obtain something, but the divine answer is always gratuitous and free from the gift of offering or sacrifice.

And it is precisely in the gift that divinity can offer mankind, in its infinite freedom, that one can find that *absolute gratuitousness* which emancipates the gift from the above-mentioned implications. Through the dynamics of the relationship, the relative dynamics of donation is also omitted. In this particular form of 'relationship', the gift from the gods is absolutely a gift of grace, a gift of love, without reason, without foundation, which can never receive an adequate response. The gift of grace is responded to, if anything, by trying to imitate that love with the power at man's disposal. What Nietzsche introduces in *Zarathustra* is a special gift, which seems to be detached from the dynamics of self-giving by placing itself in continuity with the gift of love of the God of Christians. In particular, the model of gift suggested by Nietzsche makes use of the loving relationship that sustains gratuitous giving, but clearly aims to overcome the aspects of Christian belief that he believes are no longer sustainable.

In the figure of Jesus, Christianity encapsulates the free gift that God gives to man of his son and the model to imitate so that man can in some way respond to that priceless gift. *Imitatio Christi* is therefore the happy destiny of those who, by the grace of God,[10] intend to live in God's love, in that loving relationship.

What definitively calls into question the violent dynamics of giving, and which Nietzsche felt was crucial to the overcoming he was aiming for, is the particular relationship that is established on the Christian law of love. God's love for mankind, which reaches as far as the extreme gift of Jesus, and the consequent love of mankind for God, which translates into love for the Neighbour, break the classical patterns of giving and put back into circulation the energy that nourishes the essence of the gift itself. The gift thus enters a new dimension when it frees itself from the violent dynamics that has always been inherent in the gift, to give itself to the impossible law of love.[11] Nietzsche understands the novelty of this gift, but he also understands the critical issues connected with a metaphysical vision of existence that separates the ideal world from the real world. With Zarathustra's gift, he intends to remain within this tradition by continuing it, but first of all by overcoming the difficulties that this theological conception brings with it. His immanent model cannot do without love, but such love must be perfected and revolutionized, and to do so, the distance between heaven and earth must first be bridged.[12]

The third paradigm

It has been stated how the dynamics of the gift that have just been described can in fact be attributable to a particular type of gift, namely the *munus*, and not to the gift in general, which is instead characterized by the generosity and gratuitousness with which it is made, as opposed to any other giving aimed at exchange and trade.

The value attributed by Aristotle to the gift is well known, as are his considerations on *philia* – which is based on prodigality and reciprocity among friends – and his opinion that he could not give himself *koinonìa* without friendship. Considerations that have long exerted a great influence and have undoubtedly contributed to inextricably linking the gift to spontaneity and disinterest so that it can be called such. An authentic gift would therefore be a fully altruistic gift free from the dynamics linked to the form of giving in order to take. This form of selfless giving was subsequently described by Seneca using the Latin term *beneficium* as opposed to the expression *munus*, which describes an interested and selfish gift[13] and encapsulates the obligation to repay it. Starting from this distinction we could reconstruct a twofold history of the gift, in which what prevails in the full definition of the gift par excellence is the line of the *beneficium*, back to which it seems easier to trace that spontaneity and generosity which we immediately associate with the gift. And yet *munus* and *beneficium*, more than as two distinct and separate forms of gift, appear as inseparable components of the gift in general, like inner poles that sometimes prevail over each other and sometimes balance each other, but which always remain difficult to distinguish and keep separate. However, Benveniste outlines the dynamics of give–take – which in this ideal separation we have to trace back exclusively to the gift as *munus* – already in the root **do-* and in the derivatives from the Greek *doron*, *dorea* and *dósis*, thus making it difficult even on the etymological level to isolate the authentic gift from the selfish gift. And it is always with the gift in general – and not exclusively with the form ascribable to the *munus* – that Benveniste also associates that network of meanings that refer to the insidiousness that is hidden within it and that Mauss had, in his view, highlighted through the obligation to reciprocate that the gift always imposes and through the 'force' inherent in the gift itself.

In Benveniste's articulated reconstruction, the *dósis* form is particularly significant for our discourse and for Nietzsche's use of the notion of gift. *Dósis* refers to 'the act of offering', and the expression can also take on legal meaning by translating 'the attribution of an inheritance by express will [into] attic law', but above all *dósis* refers to the medical meaning of 'dose' and 'the word served as a semantic loan in German, *Gift*, and, like the Greek and Latin *dósis*, has served as a substitute for *uenenum* "poison".[14] This refers to that insidiousness that is always hidden in the gift in general, which further confirms the ambiguity of the gift itself and the difficulty in clearly separating *beneficium* from *munus*. The gift itself is poisonous – it promises in the spontaneity with which it is offered but it can betray. The 'scandal' that the gift always constitutes for those who benefit from it lies in the necessary deciphering of that ambiguity that accompanies it. The power inherent in the gift is composed of the essence of the donor, of the relationship into which it is inserted and of the *enigma* it carries, that is, the mystery around the intentions within the donor's will to power that are transferred into the given thing. It is about a mystery that is deciphered as a poisonous gift, but which in reality hides the conflict in the will: it is about the clash between selfish will and universal will that always stirs in the human soul and reverberates in the gift. This latter, by definition, should always be spontaneous and disinterested, but in the 'scandal' it produces for the donee it reveals the ambiguity connected to it. Nietzsche explicitly uses the insidiousness of the gift and its poisonous nature in his use of the metaphor, on the one hand to show how the ambiguity that is always inherent in the donation exercises a necessary function in revealing the violent dynamics connected with gift and, on the other, to clarify how this ambiguity can be overcome when the knots that restrain the will, in the conflict between selfish will and universal will, are unravelled by love as the law that directs the will itself – and the relationships in which this will is exercised – to the overcoming of the conflict. A mechanism already unmasked by Christian love, by *agape*, yet still incapable – in Nietzsche's eyes – of a complete overcoming, since it is hampered by the distance between God and mankind, and restrained in the insuperable aporia between grace and human freedom.[15]

The albeit problematic distinction made by Seneca between *munus* and *beneficium* makes it clear, if only by contrast, that the characteristic of full gratuity must be attributed to the authentic gift – the one ascribable to *beneficium*. Starting from the assumption that such a gift can be given completely free of the dynamics of exchange, some students of Marcel Mauss, collaborating through the MAUSS – *Mouvement Anti-Utilitariste en Sciences Sociales* – have tried over the years to update and revive that concept of the gift which embraces Mauss's 'systemic' vision opposed by many precisely because of the 'big picture' aspect that is very unusual for the human and social sciences,[16] and take it in the direction, however, of an investigation aimed at highlighting the possibility of the 'gift' free from the dynamics of mere economic exchange and instead oriented towards establishing and maintaining, first of all, social relations that subsequently also incorporate economic relations. Alain Caillé in particular sees this interpretation as a 'third paradigm' for the formation of social bonds. The first paradigm, the 'utilitarian' one and the main target of the MAUSS scholars, holds 'that it is possible and at the same time necessary to refer the set of social phenomena exclusively to the decisions and calculations of individuals',[17] seen as subjects moved exclusively by the safeguarding of their own particular interests. The second paradigm, symmetrical to the first and which can be defined as 'holistic', holds instead that it can 'explain all actions, individual or collective, analysing them as manifestations of the influence exercised by the social totality on individuals and the need to reproduce it'.[18] At first one would have been tempted – observes Caillé – to inscribe in this model the gift described by Mauss, since, in continuity with his illustrious uncle Émile Durkheim, Mauss insists on the compulsoriness of the response as the predominant agent within the gift itself, thus highlighting that there can only be a gift within a pre-existing framework of reciprocity that is an overall structure of relations. Caillé and MAUSS scholars held that Mauss's investigations presented a picture that resisted the easy insertion of the gift and its dynamics into the holistic paradigm. Social totality does not pre-exist individuals, nor is the opposite true, since rather social totality, individuals and their respective positions are determined uninterruptedly and procedurally by the interrelationships and interdependencies that occur. It therefore becomes central to understand the 'generality' of this relational process. Caillé believes that it is possible to do this through a third paradigm, the paradigm of the gift, understood as the 'performer par excellence of alliances'. The space to access this interpretation of the gift is offered by Mauss himself who, although he found in every gift an obligation of repayment, overcame the holistic barriers by introducing a certain amount of freedom and individualism to accompany the eventuality and the modalities of the repayment: 'the obligation that the gift gives us is an obligation of freedom. An exhortation, one would be tempted to say, to action, in the sense that Hannah Arendt gave this term.'[19] More than a real paradigm, according to Caillé himself, this would be a path more or less consciously followed by scholars of different backgrounds and which is not ascribable to Mauss's essay *The Gift*[20] – here certainly oriented in a systematic way, in accordance with Mauss' drive – but one that is still full of questions to be verified, such as the possibility of identifying a gift that is completely free and the direction that this gift takes within society. For Caillé and Godbout there was no doubt about the possibility of identifying a completely free gift,[21] yet the very definition from which they start presents more than a few problems in an attempt to show such gratuitousness. By defining a gift as 'any supply of goods or services carried out, without a guarantee of repayment, in order to create, nourish or recreate the social bond between people',[22] it is certainly evident that there is no guarantee of repayment, but at the same time it clearly highlights the purpose for which the gift is made – the institution or preservation of social relations. The narrow definition used by Godbout and Caillé has the advantage of clarifying a dimension of the value of goods which economists seem to ignore and which goes beyond the 'value of use' and the 'value of exchange', that is with respect to the needs that a good enables to be satisfied and the quantity of other goods or the quantity of money that the good in question allows to be acquired. Through this narrow definition a further value of the good is clarified, that is the 'value of the bond', the capacity that the donated gift has to create or reproduce social relations. In spite of this appropriate extension to the 'bond value', in the definition used the obligation of repayment remains perfectly intact, since the repayment takes shape in the very relationship for which the gift is intended. And if even the possibility of reciprocating or not depends on the freedom of the individual, this does not detract from the fact that the gift thus described retains within itself the power that places the recipient before a choice from which he cannot escape. It is not by chance that Godbout – to whom Caillé refers for a clarification of the meaning of the expression – places the large and problematic paragraph dedicated to the gratuitousness of gifts immediately after the description of the 'bond value'.[23] In fact, here the question is complex to unravel. On the one hand, the gift, in order to be considered as such, must be spontaneous anddisinterested, and on the other – following Mauss – it is believed that by definition every gift awaits a recompense, be it direct or binary, that is restricted to the donor and donee, be it indirect and circular, and that is connected to a wider network of exchanges in which the repayment by the donee takes place in the society from which the donor in any case benefits. In the chapter 'Gratuità e riconoscenza' (Gratuity and gratitude) in his *Vocabulaire des institutions indo-européennes* (Dictionary of Indo-European Institutions), Benveniste effectively opens up the possibility of a gift that goes beyond the circuit of exchanges, affirming the existence of a 'second circuit, that of favour and gratitude, of what is given without waiting for a repayment, of what is offered in order to "thank"'.[24] Such a circuit could evidently be traced back to the free gift, an expression that refers to the term of religious derivation, 'grace'. The meaning of the gratuitous, disinterested gift, without a why, is an exception to the gift of exchange, to the mercantile meaning of giving, an exception that nevertheless takes place. The free gift exists as a possibility among the various forms of giving and therefore among the various economic forms. This very exception seems to suggest to Benveniste a higher level for the understanding of economic notions, which should not be trivially traced back to material needs, since 'everything that refers to economic notions is linked to much broader representations that bring into play the whole of human relations or relations with the divine; complex, difficult relations, in which the parties are always involved'.[25] The authentically free gift that goes beyond the dynamics of exchange is exclusively the gift that is inserted on a relational plane that does not allow authentic repayment. The free gift is nothing other than the form of gift that comes closest, in terms that are always and only asymptotical, to the divine gift: the authentic and only gift of 'grace'– a perfectly gratuitous and free gift in that it is animated by pure love for the person to whom it gives itself in the form of continuous creation, and a gift to which, if anything, one can respond with action aimed at continuing creation, as far as is possible for man to do and, in the Christian sense, imitating the gift that Christ himself is with gratitude: giving thanks and re-creating at the same time.

However, beyond the specifics of the Christian gift of love which Nietzsche uses for the definition of his own model of donation, what we can certainly recognize as a free gift is the initial gift from which originates the circle clearly described by the three Graces in their dance that symbolizes giving, taking and reciprocating. If the circle represented by the three Graces[26] describes a virtuous economic circuit, the greater Grace receives the first gift from which everything else proceeds without presuppositions, without conditions, without a why. It is here, if anything, that the true gratuitous, fully free and unfounded gift is, which can then lead to the virtuous, or less virtuous, circle, just as it can also remain unheeded. However, such a gift is but the mystery and sacredness of the very being in which we have always found ourselves. A condition that we can think of 'religiously', insomuch as it is precisely this condition that binds us together again in the community that recognizes itself in a common debt, as delivered to us by the Creator or in any case by an entity to which we are obliged for our very being in the world.

The difficulty of identifying the gift outside of the exchange and the circle that it activates has been highlighted, among others, by Derrida in his *Given Time*, an essay in which the philosopher reproaches Mauss for not having erased the paradox that the gift brings with it: by outlining the gift with its dynamics, with its actors and with its phenomenological characteristics, Mauss only highlighted the impossibility of the authentic and disinterested gift. Derrida clarifies that the gift, as such, can be given only in excess with respect to the exchange and circularity of giving and having, and this excess refers to time, to the event that the gift must constitute in order to be such, therefore to the events-based characteristic of the gift itself, to its unforeseen and unforeseeable happening.[27] In his discourse, Derrida also advances a juxtaposition of the 'gift' to 'nature', to *physis*, which is important for our reconstruction of Zarathustra's gift. In fact, in its double meaning of *natura naturans* and *natura naturata*, nature contains the same paradox that we associate with the gift: in an attempt to define it, it continually eludes us, 'but isn't the *phyein* of the *physis*', Derrida observes, 'above all the donation of what gives life (*donne naissance*), the original productivity that generates, causes to sprout or grow, that leads to light and blossoming?',[28] and is it therefore not here, in its possible and free happening, in its being an event, that both the authentic gift and the *physis* in its original and permanent meaning should be sought? Derrida's reflections on the gift have, among other things, the effect of making post-metaphysical, non-ontotheological, thinking possible (or, if nothing else, viable). Jean-Luc Marion[29] began his phenomenological reflections along this path. By identifying the donation, the gift, with the original phenomenon, he showed how the 'reason' for the gift (when it is such, and therefore in the beginning) cannot be reconstructed by the principle of sufficient reason. To the impossibility of the gift highlighted by Derrida, Marion responds through a phenomenological analysis of what renders the gift superimposable on the economic logic of exchange. The three figures of the 'donor', the 'donee' and the 'donated thing' contribute to rendering the gift a mere trade. Where one of these figures is missing, there would be less identification with the exchange, according to Marion, and we would be faced with a gift free from those dynamics. Beyond Marion's subtle arguments about *adonné* aimed at making a non-metaphysical phenomenology plausible on the basis of a general reflection on donation[30] and beyond the albeit significant ethical-religious consequences that his thought has had, what is useful to underline for our discourse here is essentially the thinking on the original gratuitousness of the gift of being and its necessary groundlessness, capable of suggesting a thinking beyond the foundation.

If Derrida and Marion investigate, albeit in different ways and with different outcomes, the so-called 'deconstructive' aspects of the gift and its presumed 'impossibility' and paradoxicality, then the MAUSS authors, as we have seen, follow an alternative path, which we could also define as 'constructive', highlighting the practical 'possibility' of the gift and its virtuosity. What all these attempts have in common is the identification of a 'possible' *gratuitousness* placed in the initial gift and from which everything proceeds, and it is on this form of gift that Roberto Esposito has shed new light, by other means and with other intentions, with his investigations on the origin of *communitas*.

Echoing the etymological link between *communitas* and *munus*, and appropriately insisting on the 'duty to reciprocate' which would be more marked and present in the *munus* than in the *donum* in general, Esposito clarifies how this particular form of gift-obligation holds the community together. The *munus* is the debt which has been contracted and which implies a necessary restitution; it does not indicate the gift which is received, but rather the gift which is offered: in the (duty to) give, therefore, the participants of the community are in community with each other, united by the obligation which pushes them to reciprocate one another within that community, which therefore becomes the place where the repayment takes place. What holds the community together, that is, those who are bound together in the *munus*, in the obligation, is not so much a property that they share (or possess in common), but rather the duty that they feel like a common bond: '*communitas*,' says Esposito, thus clarifying a further and fundamental distinction identified in his theoretical path,

> is the set of people united not by a 'property' but by a duty or a debt. Not by a 'more', but by a 'less', by a lack, by a limit that emerges as a burden, or even as a defective condition for the one who is, instead, 'free' or 'exempt' It is here that the [. . .] most distinguishing of the opposing duos takes shape, which accompanies or takes over from the public/private alternative: that is to say, that which puts *communitas* and *immunitas* into conflict: if *communis* is that which is obliged to perform a duty – or offer a favour – then by contrast *immunis dicitur qui nullo fungitur officio* (P. F., 127.7) and can therefore remain *ingratus*.[31]

In his counter-history of modern political thought, Esposito focuses his attention between the emergence of individuality and the *immunitas* that characterizes it as an attempt to escape from the duty that holds *communitas* together, and this is particularly interesting in relation to Nietzsche's reading of the state and its overcoming,[32] as well as for the understanding of the meaning of the 'new' possible relationships that Nietzsche hopes for using the metaphor of the gift.

Esposito observes that *munus* is at the basis of *communitas*, as a gift given, the gift that must be given to repay, and not the *donum* as a gift received. *Communitas*, understood as a group of members united in a common purpose, is not decided on the basis of a fullness, of a presence that must be shared, but of a void, of an absence that must be filled by participation in the debt. Yet the void that holds the members of *communitas* together is a response to a force that comes from nowhere. The mystery connected with this obligation that binds and re-binds the members of the community can undoubtedly be extended to the sphere of grace, as a first gift, without interest, without obligation, without a why. The free and absolute donation from which both the community and the give–take–repay circle can start. Every giving of the *munus* presupposes a having without intention, for if there were such an intention, the answer would be obligatory, while here it remains dependent on free will to join in the repayment.

Clearly, Esposito's discourse has a very clear objective that concerns the genesis and structure of society and the communities that make it up; however, the framework described presents such an extension that it examines general issues that can find an interpretation precisely from the function exercised by the gift. In fact, these considerations are particularly important in our discourse on the 'Zarathustra's gift', particularly regarding the definition of relationships in relation to the gift as *munus* and the possibility of freeing oneself from them in *immunitas*. However, these are first of all reflections that end up having a strong impact not only on the anthropological and ethical-social level, but also and above all on the ontological level[33] and that constitute a good viaticum for the further in-depth analysis of the *Weltanschauung* that Nietzsche in some way prefigures and outlines through the gift.

The 'death of God' is the announcement with which the madman sanctions in the market place the end of a certain value structure and the announcement of the possibility of a new redefinition. Nietzsche's choice of the metaphor of the gift is by no means accidental and it is by discussing *immunitas* – to extensively use Esposito's effective terminology – that the subject feels and claims in the age of the dying god that it is possible to (re)trace the path proposed by Nietzsche in the name of a new gift, a new way of giving. It is as if the question at the basis of Esposito's thesis were to be reproposed in broader terms, that is, how is it possible to inhabit human *communitas* without dissolving into it, and yet without closing oneself in the asphyxiating cage of *immunitas*?[34] In other words, how is it possible to live relationships without delegating their hold to metaphysical instances and without reducing them to the will of individuals? In order to understand and appreciate the relevance of the metaphor of the 'gift' for the entire structure of *Zarathustra*, it is necessary to focus attention on one aspect on which Nietzsche constantly insists in his work, which is, on relationships, on their constitution and on their 'renewal', since – as we have seen – it is precisely on relationships that the dynamics the gift triggers is based. In this perspective, we understand the entire narrative structure of the work and we grasp the reasons for the introduction of characters and situations that are apparently extemporaneous and deficient. It is precisely by working on the relationships and the role played in them by Zarathustra's particular 'gift', that Nietzsche clarifies some fundamental concepts both for his transvaluation of all values, since this transvaluation comes precisely through the abolition of the old values – linked to the forms of relationship that in the age of 'the death of God' show their limits because they are based on 'metaphysical' bonds that no longer hold up – and for the tension to overcome new values that become practicable through the affirmation of new forms of relationship, apparently in favour of mere *immunitas*, that are in reality as much if not more binding than the previous ones. In this picture, in which Christian love is distorted and rethought by Nietzsche and which plays a fundamental role in the definition of 'new' relationships, a number of conceptual pairs that Nietzsche opposes to underline the desired transvaluation should be read: in particular, we will see how the 'neighbour'/'friend' pair, which exemplifies the passage from evangelical love to Nietzsche's love, should be read from the point of view of the determination of a recipient who is finally ready to accept Zarathustra's gift; it is a long process of determination which also traverses the explication of another conceptual pair that is very important for the dynamics of the gift in general and for the fourth part of *Zarathustra* in particular, which is the 'enemy'/'guest' pair.

As we shall see, Zarathustra's gift is first of all directed towards 'higher men', to those who feel the unsustainable fragility of the situation in which they live and somehow push themselves to overcome it even though they are always prevented from doing so. In the fourth part of *Zarathustra*, written later than the rest of the work, the *höheren Menschen* (higher men) whom Zarathustra meets on his path come to him as 'guests' in his cave. Now, as Benveniste pointed out,[35] the theme of hospitality is closely linked to the wider field of 'giving'. The initial term for *hospes* is *hostis* and finds its correspondent in the Gothic *gasts*; but while the sense of *gasts* is 'guest', that of *hostis* is 'enemy'. To explain the relationship between 'guest' and 'enemy', it is usually acknowledged that both derive from the sense of 'foreigner', *xénox*, which is still attested in Latin, and from this we can deduce the distinction between a 'favourable foreigner' who is a 'guest' and a 'hostile foreigner' who is, in fact, an 'enemy'. It is curious that the *hostis* is not the 'foreigner' in general, but the 'foreigner' understood as the one who enters into a relationship with the 'guest' community through the exchange of gifts: as Benveniste observes explicitly using Mauss's essay *The Gift*, the foundation of the institution of hospitality is precisely the 'relationship of compensation' between host and guest:[36] here the *communis*/*immunis* pair re-appears once more, where *immunis* is the one that does not fulfil the obligation to give back and in the relationship of 'hospitality' it therefore, in the case presented by Nietzsche, becomes 'hostile', an obstacle to the overcoming and therefore destined to decline.

Through the 'honey sacrifice' (another crucial aspect, that of 'render-sacred', on which we will necessarily have to dwell), Zarathustra attracts the higher men in the hope that they will be able to reciprocate the gift that he is giving them by initiating that socio-relational dynamics functional to the new 'valorization'. Initially Zarathustra is persuaded that they know how to adequately respond to the gift, that is to say that they know how to convert the message into reality, into consequent action, in other words that they know how to donate that Over-man to Zarathustra that he prophesied, but almost immediately he realizes the inadequacy of their knowing how to donate, their insuperable limit which is founded in the metaphysical roots of their existence and is indicated in an incontrovertible way by the particular character of the 'gift' that he offers them and by the insuperable 'scandal' that it produces.

But then what exactly is this gift? And what love does Nietzsche take on as a form of relationship within which such a gift can find full realization in the dynamics it triggers?

The greatest gift

Die Feigen fallen von den Bäumen, sie sind gut und süss;
und indem sie fallen, reisst ihnen die rote Haut.
Ein Nordwind bin ich reifen Feigen.

F. Nietzsche, *Also sprach Zarathustra, Auf den glückseligen Inseln*[1]

The gift of wisdom

In the introduction to *Ecce Homo*, Nietzsche's exalted intellectual autobiography and spiritual testament, he himself describes *Thus Spoke Zarathustra* as the greatest gift (*Geschenk*) ever given to mankind,[2] a complex gift, difficult to understand,[3] always enigmatic and challenging, 'scandalizing', just as every gift is capable of being. In presenting it in these terms it is Nietzsche himself who suggests a key to the interpretation of the enigma that *Zarathustra* constitutes: it is a gift and as such demands a 'response'; but what kind? The question becomes more complicated and carries more meaning if we think that Nietzsche also defines his work as 'a sacred book', more precisely, a 'fifth Gospel'[4] with which he intends to 'challenge all religions'.[5] A gift, then, that throws down the gauntlet to all religions (does Zarathustra have a 'new' form of 'religion' in store for us?) and, by placing itself in continuity with the Gospels, intends to revise the canon in order to overcome them. It is within these parameters that one must read *Thus Spoke Zarathustra*: above of all, it is a gift that is part of the love relationship described in the Gospels in order to challenge and renew it.

When he turned thirty, Zarathustra 'left his home and the lake of his home and went into the mountains'; he abandoned his own community (his 'home'), what bound him to others, and the firm and imperturbable foundation of his bond to his community (which is the 'lake' that depicts stable and complete wealth, and remains motionless compared to a river and even more so compared to the sea, a true metaphor of the Over-man), and he retreated high into the mountains,[6] to explore in solitude the depth of his soul in the presence of nature.

From this isolation, in deep contact with nature, he drew a wisdom (*Weisheit*) that transformed him. An Emersonian echo of man's confrontation with nature – as it says in *Conduct of Life*, 'a man ought to compare advantageously with a river, an oak, or a mountain'[7] – is clear here, which Nietzsche takes up again as a pretext to explain the origin and content of the wisdom accumulated by Zarathustra and the resulting transformation that leads him to abandon his retreat, 'forcing him' in fact to give himself to men, passing on and thus communicating that wisdom. Starting with the Prologue, Zarathustra is in fact the one who, filled with riches accumulated in his retreat and *transformed* (*verwandelt*) by a wisdom that now overflows in him, needs to give himself fully, needs to become a donor and *empty himself* of that wisdom to become a man again and no longer a *transformed being*.

Like the sun that shines before him at the beginning of his journey of descent (or decline) among men, the transformed Zarathustra needs donees – he needs hands that are ready to accept the gift that he carries within himself:

> You great star! What would your happiness be if you had not those for whom you shine?
>
> [...]
>
> I want to bestow and distribute until the wise among human beings have once again enjoyed their folly, and the poor once again their wealth.
>
> For this I must descend into the depths, as you do evenings when you go behind the sea and bring light even to the underworld, you super-rich star!

[...]

Behold! This cup wants to become empty again, and Zarathustra wants to
become human again. (KSA, IV, p. 11)[8]

The similarity that Nietzsche immediately introduces with the sun at the
beginning of the Prologue clarifies without mediation the particularity of
Zarathustra's gift. It is not in fact a gesture dictated by generosity or an act
animated by moral intentions, but rather a natural requirement that has the
nature of necessity rather than free choice. Just as the sun *must* set behind the
sea in order to bring light to the underworld, in the same way Zarathustra *must*
(*muss*) 'set' among men and bring his wisdom. Just as the sun does not choose
to give its own light and warmth but is obliged to do so by its very nature, in
the same way Zarathustra must bring his gift among men, enlightening them
with that wisdom and thus transforming them. The verb used by Nietzsche
to describe the 'obligation' that motivates Zarathustra to empty himself and
to give is *müssen*, which describes a need of a natural type, and not *sollen*,
which rather refers to a moral duty. From the Prologue onwards it is clear that
Zarathustra is not moved by an ethical or pedagogical motive, but by a necessity
that comes from his deep contact, or even fusion, with nature through which
he has matured a wisdom that is such also because it compels Zarathustra to
donate and therefore move towards his decline.

Two fundamental and intimately related aspects immediately emerge. The
wisdom that has made Zarathustra a *transformed being* demands, in order
to be fully realized, the donation to men, and therefore Zarathustra cannot
preserve himself in that transformation, in that 'form' that he has temporarily
achieved but which cannot be definitive, because he is destined to being
emptied and to decline because of an insuperable intimate need for the gift
itself. Even 'Zarathustra's gift' preserves intact its motility, that is the need to
pass from hand to hand, to activate a process oriented in a certain direction.
Even this gift, which in many aspects necessarily differs from the gift we have
described in Chapter 1, has the need to activate some kind of dynamics: by

imposing a circle upon the active exchange whose effects must be understood as an integral part of the gift itself.

Another aspect that remains apparently in conformity with the usual dynamics of the gift is the *gratuitousness* that must accompany it. Although in fact Zarathustra's gift cannot be understood as a sign of generosity or liberality, neither is it accompanied by moral or philanthropic impulses, nor is it due to some form of divine 'grace', nevertheless within the necessity of Zarathustra's gift there is clearly its 'gratuity'. It is a particular gratuity, certainly, since it does not refer to an act of grace carried out by some deity who, by giving to Zarathustra, exhorts him to imitate and continue that 'gratuitous' giving; it is a gratuity that is rather to be read in this 'natural' meaning of the gift that comes to Zarathustra and from him 'must' pass to men. The will that accompanies the original transformation of Zarathustra and then the donation of this to men has nothing to do with the free choice for the good that must be communicated to men, on pain of their (and his) perdition; it has rather to do with an accumulation of potential that must be turned into will and thus pass through those who will be able to become a receptacle capable of welcoming and able, however, to empty themselves in turn or, to use another effective Nietzschean metaphor, able to become a 'bridge' towards the common tension of the Over-man. This 'natural' gratuitousness of the gift, which also involves a particular 'freedom' of the gift itself – since it reaches Zarathustra freely (freely, without a reason) and from him 'wants' to immediately go beyond without hypostatization – activates the characteristics that we normally recognize as an integral part of the act of donation.

Zarathustra's gift, like the gift in general, 'scandalizes' the recipient, forces him into some kind of response and, in the case of an acceptance, forces the recipient to respond *adequately* to the gift, to conform to that gift, and to act accordingly. In the case of Zarathustra's gift, the appropriate response is first of all to conform to the contents of that particular wisdom. Zarathustra is transformed as a result of that wisdom and seeks souls willing to make themselves chalices to fill and be immediately ready to empty themselves in order to in turn become donors of the same wisdom that transforms and leads to the decline that the Over-man announces.

The *Weisheit* of Zarathustra is clearly distinct from the *Wissen*, from the logical-deductive knowledge, and comes to Zarathustra from his retreat and isolation as the emergence of a conscious co-belonging with the totality. The moral dimension of *phronesis* and the theoretical knowledge of *sophia*, virtues that Aristotle kept separate and distinct, merge into one in the word *Weisheit*. The wisdom to which Nietzsche refers, particularly as the content of Zarathustra's gift, is the union of *phronesis* and *sophia*: a union present in the pre-Socratic thought that Zarathustra refers to as the true object of philosophy in that it is the 'love of wisdom', or continuous tension to wisdom, not as one that is separate and other from man himself, but rather as a permanent nursing of the universal bond that he feels to be constitutive of his own essence. On the other hand, the definition of the 'philosopher' in *Beyond Good and Evil*, a work that is contemporary to *Zarathustra*, is rather clear:

> A philosopher: that is a man who constantly experiences, sees, hears, suspects, hopes, and dreams extraordinary things; who is struck by his own thoughts as if they came from the outside, from above and below, as a species of events and lightning-flashes *peculiar to him*. (KSA, V, 235)[9]

The philosopher is therefore the one who thinks about what is outside of himself and knows how to recognize his own thoughts as being triggered by himself, because he recognizes in himself a common belonging to the totality and does not find that separation, typical of reflective thought, which prevents the understanding of the common origin and belonging, since starting from a gnoseological distinction creates an ontological distance that is in the end insurmountable. The wisdom that the *philo*-sopher must be constantly searching for, on the other hand, restores the unity and the common belonging of the individual to the All and makes it possible to recognize precisely in the 'love' that leads to that same wisdom the same 'love' that holds all things together; this awareness, which is never inert and static knowledge or the result of demonstrations or the mere announcements of a prophet, affects those who receive and transform it because it induces them to action in perfect conformity with that knowledge. The wisdom that Zarathustra gifts not only restitches the ontological separation between a high (from which the law comes) and a low (which conforms to this law), but also shows itself capable of holding ontology and morality together, since the action that flows from it is in perfect conformity with the more general ontological framework.

Leading the receiver to decline, the wisdom, which Zarathustra gifts, exhorts the active continuation of the law that binds the All (to which the individual, only apparently separated, always and nevertheless belongs) to oneself, which translates into the 'sacrifice' of one's own individuality. Accepting the wisdom means at the same time 'sacrificing' oneself in the name of what that wisdom augurs and promises. The theme of sacrifice is constant in *Zarathustra*, and it is not necessary to turn to the symbolic 'honey sacrifice' in Book IV to verify its presence. *Zarathustra* is a book strongly imbued with religious and biblical references in particular, and should not be trivialized as the expression of a form of neo-paganism. Undoubtedly there is a component in the work that orients it towards a form of 'new mythology', in the name of late Romantic experiences and obviously in the name of Dionysus, the great absentee of the work who evidently, however, precisely through his absence testifies to his constant presence as a horizon of reference within which this new mythology must unfold and *take place*.[10] However, the religiosity of *Zarathustra* is rather to be read as a tension to overcome Christianity,[11] which is not, however, accomplished through the simple return to a form of paganism or through a Feuerbachian reversal in which the (over?)man (re)absorbs the characteristics that he once attributed to the God who is now dying, but who, on the contrary, cannot disregard Christian tradition and who also intends to accept the law of love within a framework that is, however, no longer cut away from metaphysics (which distinguishes an ideal world and an apparent world), but rather is a form of immanent transcendence that takes on the human dimension in a natural context but leaves no room for reductionist solutions either in the spiritualistic or the naturalistic sense. What allows this perilous equilibrium is precisely the unexhausted tension of the Over-man, a tension that is never exhausted and that activates a constant process of overcoming or transcending oneself, that is, one's own individuality. But beyond these general considerations, the religiosity of *Zarathustra* is testified, as already said, by the presence of the theme of sacrifice. Zarathustra himself is a sacrificial figure. Both an officiant and a sacrificial victim, he himself is the chalice (*Becher*) that empties out the accumulated wisdom, in an obvious analogy to the wine transformed into the blood of Christ by Christ himself in the dual role as mediator of the transformation by the will of God and as the lamb of the sacrifice chosen by God for men. Zarathustra's sacrifice is through the necessary abandonment of that fusion with nature matured in his isolation and is realized in his decline among men. The *Untergang* to which he is destined is a necessary step to be taken. There is neither glory nor kindness in that gesture; the will that determines it is not the expression of a moral action freed from the laws that govern the totality, but rather from the accumulated potency (in the sense of ability, of capability/know-how) and not from a decision taken deliberately on the basis of ethical considerations, which seem to interrupt the flow of events constituting the exception. It is therefore certainly a necessary decision, but is not the choice of Christ also necessary? This natural necessity seems here, in *Thus Spoke Zarathustra*, to be superimposed on the necessity of Christ's sacrifice and even to want to undermine it. The Crucified sacrifices Himself for the necessity willed by God, but on several occasions Jesus manifests a resistance to fulfilling the task assigned to Him. Not only the 'take this cup from me' (Lk. 22.42) pronounced by Jesus at the Mount of Olives as his fatal destiny approaches, but above all the crucial 'My God, my God, why have you forsaken me' (Mk 15.34) pronounced on the Cross and on which so much has been written and debated. Obviously, without the luxury of further investigation here into issues that would take us away from the problem that we want to focus on, it nevertheless seems that we do not find similar resistance in Zarathustra, a resistance that strongly attests to the humanity of Christ, his fragilities that bring him closer to us and therefore confirm his sacrifice 'for us'. The 'human, too human' resistance of Christ is not present in Zarathustra, who on the contrary does everything to fulfil his destiny, to become his own destiny, to accelerate and make possible the realization of the pernicious wisdom for him and for the individuality of those who will receive it. It is as if the will that in Jesus is still divided and asks for a solution through the Father's love to keep it united, has, in the wisdom of Zarathustra, found reconciliation. In the evangelical passages we have mentioned, in fact, the 'resistance' of Christ the man is not simply present, but rather the separation between the human will and the divine or universal will is highlighted: a conflict which is always present in man and which requires love, or rather the 'will to love', in order to structure itself adequately. In Luke's Gospel, in fact, we read: 'Father, if you are willing, take this cup from me', and already in the very brief clause 'if you are willing' there is a free will that leads to the necessary sacrifice but is capable of arresting its destiny with a free choice; but above all we read immediately afterwards in the words of Jesus a further clarification of the moment and the nature of the necessity that looms: 'yet not my will, but yours be done.' Here it is clear that we are faced with a double will, the will of the man Jesus who, on the one hand, expresses his humanity with the fear of the approaching fatal hour and with the will to preserve himself in his own individuality and, on the other hand, who recognizes a higher will – that of God – to which he surrenders himself even with suffering and which will lead him to overcome the simply human condition.[12] In Zarathustra there is no such division of the will. Since his descent among men, it is as if the will of his own wisdom used him as herald and donor. It is as if in the *transformed* Zarathustra the knots of the will had been untied and resolved by the love for the All. At the beginning of his retreat he obeyed his own individual will and chose isolation and retreat; he certainly ran the risk of losing himself in that isolation and in his subjectivity,[13] but from there he drew that wisdom which instead put him back in harmony with the totality and exhorted him to communicate the common bond to all.

The even more enigmatic expression '*Eloi, Eloi, lema sabachthani?*' ('My God, my God, why have you forsaken me?'), with which Jesus takes up the first words of Psalm 22 [21] bears further witness to this tragic separation between the will of man and divine will which must find reconciliation on the Cross and then naturally in the resurrection. It is certainly not enough to enumerate the passages in which Jesus clarifies his communion with God's will[14] in order to eliminate the internal conflict with the human will cried out from the Cross. This rift remains in man and the sacrifice of Christ and his resurrection mark the path that the 'free' will of each person 'must' take to heal the conflict and untie the knots of the will in the name of love, so that it may be fully the 'will to love'. But the rift to be healed and the knots of the will to be untied are the result of an original ontological distinction that determines them, namely the separation between God and man (and by extension – not trivial for Christianity – between God and creation). God's love for mankind, which translates not only into creation but into the ultimate gift of His Son, signals to mankind the way forward. His gift offers an example to respond to and conform to in order to approach that love (in *Imitatio Christi*), but human effort will always be incapable of that 'perfection' and will always and in any case be translated into an aspiration, helped by grace but prevented by sin, which if anything will be fulfilled in the afterlife. Zarathustra also exhorts a full love that will find fulfillment in the Over-man, thus attesting to the impossibility of 'fully' reaching that fullness that it represents. However, Zarathustra is totally pervaded by a love that knows no otherness and that in fact makes it possible for man – with his own strength alone – to resolve and overcome the knots of the will by adhering to a single will that always gives and never holds anything back for itself, and the impossibility of reaching the Over-man lies in the need for those who set out in that direction to renounce themselves, so that from *their own* decline can the *Übermensch* be born, which they will never be able to see with *their* own eyes.

It has been opportunely observed that the physical-natural aspect of Zarathustra's gift is to be understood as an alternative put forward by Nietzsche to the Christian gift of love.[15] However, believing that Nietzsche wants to replace that love as the law of donation – and of the relationships on which it is grafted or determined – with a simple physical-natural necessity does not allow one to grasp the authentic meaning of the introduction of the gift in the particular context described by Nietzsche himself as the 'fifth-Gospel'. Nietzsche's intention is far more structured and complex than simply abolishing the law of love by introducing a naturalistic reductionist model. In fact, if that were the case, one would not understand the need for constant recourse to the gift, but above all one would not understand the continuous reference to the dynamics that always accompanied the gift. Rather than abolishing the law of love, through the use of the extraordinarily rich metaphorical framework of the gift, Nietzsche aims to 'perfect' that law, replacing the old tables with the new ones that also, necessarily, fit into that course of action. Only in this way, however, is it possible to grasp, on the one hand, the authentic meaning of the expression the 'fifth Gospel' and, on the other, the insistence on the gift as a means of communicating wisdom. Why talk about 'fifth' in a series if there is no continuity, but distinct and abrupt interruption? Why speak of the 'fifth-Gospel' if there is no trace in it of the law of love that characterizes the New Testament and, if, at most, the references to it are simply aimed at its abolition and overcoming? And why choose as a way of communicating wisdom the gift with all the implications that it brings with it and with all that it evokes in reference to its gratuitousness and therefore the bond with the 'grace' (*gratia*) that animates it? Why not simply talk about a new doctrine to teach, to communicate, or even to demonstrate rationally? Why, then, have recourse to a dynamics that is in direct continuity with the love of the New Testament and which implies a general rethinking of the relationships within which it acts, if this continuity is to be simply eliminated and abandoned?

It has been said that the gift, whatever it may be, is nourished by the relationship that it insists on (or that it helps to establish) and there is no gift that does not affect the relationship between donor and donee. Hence the choice made by Nietzsche to use the dynamics of giving as a central instrument for rethinking the law of love of the Gospels: a law on which both God's relationship with mankind and men's relationships with each other is based, which, from the point of view of overcoming it, cannot simply be 'taken away' (and an incontrovertible sign of this impossibility is precisely the use of the gift, which immediately evokes God's *agape* love for mankind), but must if anything be overturned, rethought, and renewed in a framework (the one described by the 'death of God') in which the relationship to the Other is 'taken away' – this yes – and therefore also the distance between the earthly world and the heavenly world. This in no way means denying or abolishing love; it simply means perfecting it in the light of a new awareness. In this upheaval of the relational plane the particular type of gift used by Nietzsche[16] cannot in any way be neglected – nor can a consideration be undervalued, which he himself hoped for in *Ecce Homo* – regarding the choice of the donor, which rests precisely on the 'prophet' Zarathustra. But before a reflection on Zarathustra and the reasons that probably led Nietzsche to choose the Iranian prophet as his donor, it is necessary to clarify the nature of the gift he brings to mankind.

It is immediately clear that Zarathustra's gift is a gift of wisdom (*Weisheit*): in fact, it is a proclamation, a message that he must 'communicate', but that he must first of all 'give'. Transformed by the wisdom he received in his isolation, Zarathustra is 'weary of [his] wisdom, like a bee that has gathered too much honey. [He] need[s] hands that reach out.' The wisdom that he brings as a gift cannot remain inert in the hands of those who acquire it; not even Zarathustra can keep that wisdom for himself, for in order for him to keep the promise he is making, it must also be given and, only in this particular way, communicated. In his gift, he announces/teaches the Over-man, the Übermensch, and the way to him. Zarathustra's message originally reached his own ears by itself: the wisdom that now overflows in his heart is not the result of scientific demonstrations or logical deductions, but comes to him in a completely 'free' and groundless way from his absolute isolation and contact with nature. Now that his wisdom has matured in him, Zarathustra is forced to empty himself, but the very necessity that moves him to empty himself of that wisdom drives him to do so in the way that comes closest to the way in which that wisdom came to him. Just as the wisdom of the Over-man came to Zarathustra originally and without reason as a gift, so, in a similar way, he must now 'give back', disoblige himself, empty himself of that wisdom, giving it to men. The modalities of the reception will obviously depend on how many are able to accept the role and function of benefactors of this particular gift, but the practice of donation by Zarathustra will remain constant from the beginning to the end of the book.

The wisdom that Zarathustra's gift brings with it rests on the senselessness of the world, on its abyssal nature, which is now shown historically with the event of the 'death of God'. The gift offered by Zarathustra consists of a wisdom aimed at salvation from that desperate senselessness into which the world declines. Certainly, this gift lies in the idea of the Over-man that is suggested and in the doctrine of eternal recurrence as the 'heaviest' hypothesis, but what actually constitutes the essence of that wisdom lies rather in both the idea that it is possible to 'give meaning' to senseless existence – that is, it is possible to choose the tension to the Over-man and the acceptance of the eternal recurrence[17] – and that man's destiny does not consist in the simple alternative between oblivion – that is, the 'removal' of the groundlessness and insignificance of existence – and the desperate surrender to passive, declining nihilism.

> Once the sacrilege against God was the greatest sacrilege, but God died,
> and then all these desecrators died. Now to desecrate the earth is the most

terrible thing, and to esteem the bowels of the unfathomable higher than the meaning of the earth! (KSA, IV, 15)[18]

Sacrilege now means, in the era of the 'death of God', to turn one's hopes to the unfathomable, to transcendence, to the afterlife, hoping to derive from it the meaning of our existence. The wisdom that Zarathustra now intends to give to men consists in the awareness that he can 'create' with his own strength, that he can 'give meaning' to the earth from within that senselessness into which the world appears to have fallen ('perhaps there has never yet been such an "open sea"' (KSA, III, 574).[19] 'Behold, I teach you the overman! [. . .] Let your will say: the overman shall be the meaning of the earth!' proclaims Zarathustra to the crowd gathered in the market square, in a manner not unlike the announcement with which the *madman* proclaims the 'death of God' in *The Gay Science*. And yet, shortly before, in the very first lines in which he simply hints at his wisdom, Zarathustra reveals the mystery hidden in this novella and makes it completely different from the unprecedented communication of the *madman*. The context is similar, but the content of the message is absolutely different. While the 'death of God' may be announced by the *madman* behind whom the historical figure of Diogenes of Sinope probably lies, and may in fact remain an unheard message, since it does not yet require a 'positive' reaction, the wisdom that Zarathustra wants to communicate, precisely because it claims to be the condition for overcoming the abyss opened by the 'death of God' and therefore the 'positive' response to the passive nihilistic shift,[20] requires a mode of communication that does not leave one indifferent, that even scandalizes and that obliges one to respond in some way, and the gift fulfills this function in full.

Gift of love

The gift lends itself perfectly to this need inherent in the content of the wisdom that pervades Zarathustra completely, since, on the one hand, in accordance with the usual dynamics that are inherent in it and which we have outlined, it forces the donee to respond in some way, and, on the other hand, it immediately inserts that unheard-of communication into a precise tradition – which is dying with God, who is first and foremost for Nietzsche the God of the Christians – in perfect continuity with it. The first dialogue that Zarathustra held on his descent from the mountains bears witness to this in an incontrovertible way. This was the exchange with the holy hermit whom Zarathustra had already met years before on his ascent when he chose his isolation and who now, seeing him coming down from his mountain, immediately recognizes him as a *transformed being*. Assuming the hermit to have the same feeling that pervades him, Zarathustra clearly affirms his desire to return among men to give them a gift (*ein Geschenk*). But this greatly amazes the hermit, who in his retreat instead of love for men, matured love for God and expects, in turn, that isolation will have had the same effect on Zarathustra. 'I love men', says Zarathustra, revealing his intentions, but the saint does not understand: that 'same' love for men, the saint says, had led him to his retreat, but from that experience he had not seen his love for men reconfirmed and increased; rather, he had arrived at his love for God: 'Now I love God: human beings I do not love. Human beings are too imperfect a thing for me.' It is precisely the love that had driven the holy hermit to isolation that Nietzsche, through *Zarathustra*, intends to distort and renew, because it comes from the metaphysical relationship that binds God to men and always leads to separation and detachment – the saint's love for God is nothing more than the perfect 'spiritualization' of that love and the consequent great contempt for man and his imperfection in the face of the Ideal. Listening with amazement to the words of the hermit who evidently did not receive the news of the 'death of God' ('[c]ould it be possible! This old saint in his woods has not yet heard the news that God is dead!'), Zarathustra understands that in order to communicate his wisdom it is necessary to rethink the relationship between men in the light of that awareness and therefore it is necessary to reform love so that it becomes the law of that renewed relationship. But the soil is not yet ready for sowing, 'Why did I speak of love?' Zarathustra almost reproaches himself for having revealed the most secret intention of his announcement, 'I bring mankind a gift', he corrects himself but only partially, since the holy hermit himself warns him at once about the risks associated with the gift: 'Give them nothing,' the hermit cautions. 'Rather take something off them [. . .] And if you want to give to them, then give nothing more than alms, and make them beg for that too!' The hermit knows perfectly well the secret behind the gift; he knows that it is intended to renew God's love (as *agape*) for mankind, but his great contempt for man – matured within the nefarious metaphysical separation between the real world and the apparent world on which his 'spiritualization' and his loneliness feeds – prevents him from admitting the possibility of a donee capable of recognizing the authenticity of giving. Men can at most be given 'alms', since they simply have the role of supplicant subjects who must constantly recognize their inferiority. However, Zarathustra is not willing to give alms, '[f]or that I am not poor enough,' he says – that is, he does not see himself in a position of presumed superiority, since this always feeds off the above-mentioned separation and Zarathustra has indeed overcome it in his isolation from which he has 'gratuitously' gained his wisdom. The holy hermit, the expression and metaphor of blind faith in metaphysical separation, has misunderstood even his own isolation in which he revels in praising God in communion with nature but in total contempt for man, in whom he no longer has any faith whatsoever. 'Then see to it that they accept your treasures! They are mistrustful of hermits and do not believe that we come to give gifts' – the old saint recognizes himself in the ranks of hermits who are ready to give their wisdom, their treasures, though to a world that in his eyes is unable to appreciate the benefit. In his contempt for man and in the illusion of repaying God's love for man with his retreat 'singing, weeping, laughing and growling I praise the god who is my god', the hermit only reveals the lie in which he leads his existence in the love for the transcendent, and cannot understand the value within Zarathustra's gift, who clearly warns that his message cannot reach those ears, because it completely distorts the vision in which the hermit leads his life: 'What would I have to give you! But let me leave quickly before I take something from you!' Zarathustra knows that his gift will sweep away the hermit's beliefs, but at the same time he fears that from those certainties, rooted in the isolation in which the hermit – like him – lived, he may in turn be contaminated. Risk always lurks in the gift, and the hermit with his rule of life promises to give an afterlife happiness. Zarathustra fears that by remaining with him in a relationship of 'hospitality', the old man may give Zarathustra the gift of that metaphysical wisdom and that he will therefore enclose himself in his isolation, in the appearance of his fullness and perfection, and may resist the need to give to men who had led him to abandon his mountain. That is why he quickly takes leave of the holy 'tempter' in a symbolic stepping down, and goes among men to bring a new gift, clarifying how the original contact with nature from which the gift itself comes cannot in any way be resolved in the solitude of contemplation, but that wisdom requires that from the confrontation with nature matures the renewed relationship of love for men and between men, and from there the need to rethink, broaden and turn upside down the love of the God of Christians. By claiming to love man, Zarathustra intends to unmask that love which is based on God's lie and establish love relationships between men, starting with the illusion that they derive their origin from God's love. According to Zarathustra, love for man means the substitution of that metaphysical subject with the immanent love of which Zarathustra becomes a prophet.

Zarathustra does not, however, intend to abolish Christian love, but rather to use the dynamics on which it has prospered for centuries to replace it with an affirmative love which, by abolishing the distance between God and men (as imperfect imitators of that love which always comes from God), brings that love back to earth, *orienting* it to the Over-man, as the infinite and common tension of men to their own overcoming. It is undeniable that at least apparently the identification of a common end as the goal of that love is in continuity with the love of Christians completely oriented towards perfection in the kingdom of heaven. What is missing here, however, is an inscrutable origin from which that love and that drive would come – in short, the metaphysical distinction is missing and with it comes discredit and contempt for the imperfections of man, who can now carry the weight of their choices on their shoulders. Within that separation from the transcendent, it is as much as possible a compassionate love for man, while Zarathustra, whose wisdom does not feed on metaphysical separation and does not live on contempt for men, teaches with his gift a love that can re-bind them once more and orient them, finally, towards the common *Streben* towards the Over-man. This wisdom comes from the earth itself, that is, from the fate to which we are bound and which we can love once more; this wisdom comes precisely from the common belonging of men to the world, that is, from the totality from which the metaphysical conception kept them separated, stained with a sin that prevented them from fully adhering to the All. Paradoxically, the same lie of God's that once held men together in the common obligation to give back and give thanks for their being-in-the-world willed by God, now renders them – in the age of 'the death of God' – 'exempt' from that bond; knowing that God no longer exists and is no longer the foundation and guide for man, gives man a sense of bewilderment which, on the one hand, beguiles him with the lure of his finally 'rediscovered' independence and, on the other hand, literally destines him to despair, to the absence of hope, in a sense, of existence. In fact, there is no hope for those who simply think the resources for the affirmation of their own existence lie in themselves; who else but a madman could think the ultimate answers for their own being in the world lie in in their loneliness (in the sense of *immunitas* which frees them from the common bond of *communitas*) and in their autonomy? Zarathustra's gift offers a wisdom capable of orienting the overcoming of that nihilistic *immunitas*, but it does not lead to a joyful and definitive *communitas*; not at all, in fact in the gift that Zarathustra has in store there is the very emptying of the bond: the end of that common restitution is in fact the decline of man, so that from this decline what is beyond-man may be born. Zarathustra therefore uses the gift and the law of renewed love to go beyond the gift itself or beyond its dynamics, to unmask the mechanism behind its 'gratuitousness' and lead mankind into its destiny of decline, a destiny that responds to a greater love that is love for the All, that is, love for eternity, if we understand by eternity not an infinite time but the fullness of being[21] that reveals itself in the moment.

With respect to the gift of the Christian tradition, which is proclaimed above all as a gift (of love) from God to men, who must give back in an infinite effort by remaining within the love of God (Jn 15.10: '[i]f you keep my commands, you will remain in my love, just as I have kept my Father's commands and remain in his love'),[22] Zarathustra's gift does not depend on an original donor – Zarathustra himself is a simple mediator – and his strength and power depend on the gift itself. However, this does not take away from the fact that Zarathustra's gift continues to be tied to 'restitution'; the gift of wisdom is in no way disconnected from the relationship between donor and donee – the relationship is simply revolutionized in the light of the specificity of the gift and its dynamics. The wisdom that is given through Zarathustra imposes on the one who receives it an adequate response whose norm is inscribed in the very wisdom that remains. The gift 'scandalizes', however, not because the donee must feel an obligation to the *prophet* Zarathustra, who literally carries the word 'of others' (or rather, 'of other') and becomes a simple mediator; the obligation of restitution that the gift imposes derives from the absence of a separate *auctoritas* rather than from the *auctoritas* from which it comes. The wisdom that is now being given comes completely gratuitously to Zarathustra, like the rising to the surface of a common knowledge, of a belonging that has always bound us to the totality. Even more binding is therefore this obligation as opposed to an obligation contracted with a God to whom we could never fully correspond in an adequate manner. Zarathustra's gift is, after all, a voice that we have always heard within us, and it is the voice that communicates our common root to us, our common origin that binds us to the totality and is able to re-bind, to realign the selfish will to the universal will towards our common destiny. This is according to a thought that presents a clear Emersonian echo and refers to Nietzsche's very first philosophical writings,[23] but which in Nietzsche's later philosophy is clarified as an inexhaustible tension to the Over-man, understood as an alternative to the passive nihilistic destiny of 'the last man'. With the 'death of God', a clear and unmediated alternative opens up between a destiny that continues the desperate declination that has led to the breakdown of the hypothesis of God – who for centuries fulfilled His function as community bond (in the highest and widest sense of the expression) – and the choice for an active nihilism that acknowledges the absence of ultimate foundations and chooses the destiny of overcoming the desperate declination to which the being seems to have been consigned in the era of the 'death of God'. This resolution comes, as said, through the acceptance of a new affirmative love that supplants the love of the compassionate and intends to deliver every dispersed fragment to the totality from which it is separated. It is from here that it is possible to derive the understanding of those final exhortations to the new love which can be read in §4 of the Prologue and which outside of this theoretical context are contradictory and paradoxical:

> What is great about human beings is that they are a bridge and not a purpose: what is lovable about human beings is that they are a *crossing over* and a *going under*.
>
> [. . .]
>
> I love those who do not first seek behind the stars for a reason to go under and be a sacrifice, who instead sacrifice themselves for the earth, so that the earth may one day become the overman's.
>
> [. . .]
>
> I love the one who makes of his virtue his desire and his doom: thus for the sake of his virtue he wants to live on and to live no more.
>
> [. . .]

I love the one whose soul squanders itself, who wants no thanks and gives none back: for he always gives and does not want to preserve himself.

[. . .]

I love the one whose soul is overfull, so that he forgets himself, and all things are in him: thus all things become his going under. (KSA, IV, 16–18)[24]

This articulated profession of love pronounced by Zarathustra with a clear reference to the Beatitudes[25] opens with a premise that anticipates and summarizes each subsequent assertion. The love for man that Zarathustra professes is a love aimed above all at liberating man from himself, from his subjectivity, from the cage of finitude within which he had found comfort as a privileged channel for contact with God, to whom he gave thanks. Among the effects of Christianity against which he intends to direct the love brought as a gift by Zarathustra, there is in fact the exasperation of subjectivity which, starting from the mediation of the absolute operated by Christ-man, leads within modernity, in an inextricable interweaving with the process of secularization, to an exasperation of the value assigned to the individual and to forms of intimate religiosity which end up denying the very meaning of religion, understood as re-*legere*, keeping together. The paradoxical effect of misunderstood Christianity is in fact the strengthening of the subject: think of the impudent attitude of those who listen in the market square, firm in their convictions, in their 'subjectivity', in the illusion of being sheltered from collapse, to the *madman* who announces the 'death of God'. Those who claim to understand the Over-man as the empowerment of the individual do not grasp the alternative proposal to this destiny of decline that Nietzsche puts forward instead. Rather than the strengthening of the individual, the Over-man foreshadows the abandonment of individuality; what is worthy of love in man is not his capacity to strengthen himself, but rather his capacity to give up that power, to renounce coming to an end in order to become a means of overcoming. What is worthy of love in man is his capacity to 'detach himself' from himself, to empty himself of his own power (or rather of this illusion) and to take (the appropriate) step back, to exonerate himself from the environment in which he is immersed and from the impulses that come from him.[26] Man is an animal 'not yet firmly determined' (*festgestellt*) – we read in §62 of *Beyond Good and Evil* – and in this lies his condemnation and at the same time his fortune, because he is not closed within an environment (not only biologically speaking, but also fully ontologically) that determines and defines him in a final form to be realized. His eventual *entelechy* is always open to different solutions: what Nietzsche hopes for through Zarathustra is that man will recognize in his own 'potentiality' not an end to be fulfilled in the strengthening of his own individuality, but a means to convert that potential into a tension to overcome the individual condition. The love that Zarathustra professes in the Prologue is intended to show this resource in man and is aimed at awakening this deep feeling, always present in the depths of his soul as a capacity to 'detach' from himself, from the cage of his own individuality, to feel part of an ever-becoming totality to which man has always belonged. By declaring his love, Zarathustra does nothing more than recall that tie of the bond that binds us to the All and which, although it is harboured in the ground of our soul, needs to be awakened, because the metaphysical coating has carved out such a deep separation that we are deluded about our autonomy and self-sufficiency. With the figure of the God who became man and with the love that accompanies this particular 'gift', Christianity certainly set out on this path, which leads to the overcoming of distinctions, but it remained prisoner of the metaphysical separation on which it was founded and of the theological constructions that were built on it, progressively determining, on the one hand, the insignificance of the hypothesis of God and therefore His historical 'death' and, on the other, the strengthening of subjectivity which, nourished by the metaphysical separation, accumulated in itself that value attributed and assigned a time outside of itself, with God. 'The fact that God became man,' observed Nietzsche in *Freedom of Will and Fate*, 'only reminds us that man must not seek his bliss in the infinite, but must found his paradise on earth.'[27]

It is certainly paradoxical, but among the effects of this decisive step taken by Christianity which shows God becoming man, there is the flip side of the coin: it is man who made himself God. By not abolishing the original distinction between the ideal world and the real world, man deludes himself into (re) appropriating those attributes he had reserved for God, and he does not grasp the authentic message, which according to Nietzsche is at the basis of the law of love of the Gospels. As he himself shows many years later in a decisive passage in *The Antichrist*, the love of the Gospels aims at the realization of bliss directly 'on earth' by overcoming all distinctions, including of course the fundamental distinction between 'true world' and 'apparent world':

> [T]he incapacity for resistance here becomes morality ('resist not evil:' the profoundest saying of the Gospels, in a certain sense, the key to them), blessedness in peace, in gentleness, in *inability* to be hostile. What is 'glad tidings?' True life, eternal life has been found – it is not promised, it is there, it is *in you*: as life in love, in love without abatement, and exemption, without distance. (KSA, VI, 200)[28]

The constitutive and characteristic aspects of the original evangelical love echo in the still distant figure of the *Übermensch*:[29] it is in fact a love that knows no distinctions and from which nothing is taken away, a love that is always devoid of resentment and revenge, 'it does not find fault, it does not offer resistance; it does not bring "the sword"'. However, the love of the Gospels, according to Nietzsche, is not in itself sufficient for the overcoming and in fact leads on the one hand to nihilistic indifference and on the other to the exaltation of individuality. With his 'fifth Gospel', Nietzsche believes he can take that 'decisive step' in the direction already marked by the love of the Gospels, capable of overcoming the shoals into which historical Christianity has led. The love of the Gospels must be integrated with an *active dynamics* that is able to (re)constitute it from within as an infinite *positive will to create*, to 'give meaning' where meaning is lost and abandoned to a perpetual decline. This 'positive' aspect is, according to Nietzsche, absent in the love of Jesus, which presents itself rather as a passive or, at best, simply 'reactive' attitude.

Nietzsche believes that in the *can*-not-be-enemies of the evangelical word lies the necessary but not sufficient premise for that total love which is love for the *Übermensch*. The 'glad tidings' show us the possibility of realizing our *life* on earth in the heart of our soul; it ultimately shows us that bliss is possible 'here and now', 'as life in love without distinctions or exclusions'. According to Nietzsche, however, this announcement is made within a religious-metaphysical context which ends up resolving the emancipation drive and does not achieve what it promises.

To accept and understand such a preliminary wisdom (*Weisheit*) means, however, to set out on the long road of love that leads to the *Übermensch*, to the 'new' meaning to be assigned to the earth, but for this to be realized, a 'new love', a renewed love, is needed, which is precisely what Zarathustra has professed since the Prologue.

In clarifying the nature of this love, Zarathustra reveals it as an authentic exhortation to action ('*die höchste That*') within a new dynamics of giving: 'I love the one who squanders its own soul', Zarathustra reiterates, taking up again the passage above in which he praised the one able to sacrifice himself without the need to 'seek behind the stars for a reason', but 'sacrifice themselves for the earth, so that the earth may one day become the overman's'. However, in this renewal he clarifies a precise dynamics. Zarathustra does not simply call for self-sacrifice, but rather shows how this sacrifice must be made in order for it to serve its purpose. The sacrifice is in fact made in the gift that one makes of oneself, of *one's own* wealth, of *one's own* goods, of *one's own* individuality, without, however, in any way wanting to trigger *for oneself* the mechanism of reward-restitution. In fact, whoever 'wants no thanks and gives none back' is worthy of love, that is to say, he who frees himself and is freed from the gift understood as an exchange,[30] because he is capable of separating himself from *his* goods first of all by disposing of his own *self*, 'whose soul squanders itself'.

He becomes worthy of this love because he always gives and does not want to keep himself and in so doing he is not a 'donor' who demands benefits, nor a 'donee' who reciprocates, but a simple means and instrument of that donation, which is the authentic Subject of this dynamics that has the birth of the *Übermensch* as its aim. Here Zarathustra offers an additional access key to the mechanism hidden in the narrative and argumentative structure of the work. The love which Zarathustra is filled with, and which he now intends to give in the form of wisdom that leads to the Over-man, is the 'law' according to which the new relationships must be established: virtuous, in fact, is he who acts according to this law. The virtue introduced in the Prologue in this profession of love and then taken up again later in a speech entirely dedicated to it is precisely the 'bestowing virtue'. A single virtue must guide man, because in this *schenkende Tugend* the knots of the will are resolved that prevent the adherence to the love which Zarathustra exhorts, and enclose the individual in *his own* will, 'shrinking him'. The 'bestowing virtue' instead translates that higher will into which the selfish will must flow:

> When you are the ones who will with a single will, and this turning point of all need points to your necessity: there is the origin of your virtue.
>
> Indeed, it is a new good and evil! Indeed, a new, deep rushing and the voice of a new spring!
>
> It is power, this new virtue; it is a ruling thought and around it a wise soul: a golden sun and around it the snake of knowledge. (KSA, IV, 99)[31]

In this 'bestowing virtue', for the love of which one wants at the same time to 'live on and to live no more', lies the enigma that accompanies Zarathustra's gift, and which in the passage just mentioned echoes in the figure of the serpent around the golden sun, the image of which refers to the poisonous nature of the gift that alludes on the one hand to the 'selection' of the right donee and on the other to the 'perdition' to which they are subjected. The figure of the snake returns, for that matter, in a rather significant way in 'On the Vision and the Riddle', one of Zarathustra's best-known and most interpreted speeches,[32] in which the nature of the gift of wisdom is hidden behind an *enigma* (also always insidious and challenging) to be resolved. The figure of the serpent penetrating the shepherd's throat seems to represent a poisonous wisdom (because it is *poisoned*, that is, misunderstood and betrayed), deadly in itself, which can however be reconverted through a decision, a 'detachment' that must take place so that the poisonous (and poisoned)[33] gift of wisdom can be properly accepted. The shepherd (of flocks? – a reference, perhaps, to the preaching of Christ – see Jn 10.1-21 – and to his possible ability to re-convert a now poisoned doctrine?) biting off the serpent's head 'transforms' him into the Over-man, within whom the perfection of the love for the all, prefigured by the eternal recurrence of the same, is attained.

Beyond these considerations, it is enough here to hold firm how the 'bestowing virtue' is able to translate in 'ethical' terms the action of those who conform to the dynamics (first of all 'ontological') of love suggested by Zarathustra.

The introduction of a 'virtue', and therefore of an ethical connotation in the choice that is made by conforming to it or not, clarifies how the exhortation to give that echoes in these pages is not a mere invitation to 'squander' one's soul, to empty it of all content and to devote oneself to a continuous expenditure of energy. The emptying of one's soul, to which Zarathustra exhorts, does not end in this continuous giving of oneself 'without reason', as the Nietzschean intent has sometimes been understood to assume in the sense, for example, of the *dépense* suggested by Bataille – an aspect which is also present in Nietzsche and which highlights the limits of an economic conception reduced to the law of profit. In *Zarathustra*, the gift, the expenditure of self is not, however, an end in itself; in this emptying there is rather constantly an end towards which this surplus and excess should be directed, and this end is precisely the Over-man. Zarathustra does not simply love those who are ready to 'squander' their overcrowded souls, those who are ready to sacrifice themselves to become weariless donors. He loves first of all what is 'great about human beings', namely the fact that they – precisely because of their undefined character – know how to be a 'a bridge and not a purpose' ('what is lovable about human beings is that they are a *crossing over* and a *going under* [*Untergang*]'). In his giving of himself, man prepares his own end (*Untergang*) as a 'crossing over' (*Übergang*) to the Over-man and therefore his giving must not simply turn into a chaotic expenditure of energy. His giving of himself becomes 'virtuous' when he conforms his own will to the only will (to power) oriented to the overcoming of every individuation, because from that dynamics, which he 'virtuously' takes for himself, every dispersed fragment is included in the totality. He whose soul is overflowing and of such wealth does not use it to increase his own power, but rather makes use of it to direct it towards overcoming himself, obeying to the utmost the 'bestowing virtue': he makes himself one with the will to power, but not simply for the purpose of a continuous excess, but to act *ethically* (hence the use of the expression 'virtue' which refers to moral action) in the direction of the Over-man.

3

For whom the sun shines

Had I not seen the Sun
I could have borne the shade
But Light a newer Wilderness
My Wilderness has made

E. Dickinson[1]

Donors and donees

Staying with the story in *Zarathustra*, the idea of the Over-man, of the *Übermensch* – this is the idea that initially dominates the work and only later is it integrated with the hypothesis of the eternal recurrence of the same – is something that is offered to him, it is an image that reaches him. The message would remain inert if Zarathustra were to keep it for himself, or rather, it would affect his own health as well as the solidity of the image of the Over-man, which would become blurred and 'deformed', as shown by the mirror belonging to the child in the revelatory dream that opens the book. Zarathustra has returned again to the mountain waiting to see the results of his 'sowing' among men, but in his new and long isolation he realizes what danger his wisdom runs:

> What frightened me so in my dream that it waked me? Did not a child approach me carrying a mirror?
> 'Oh Zarathustra' – spoke the child to me – 'look at yourself in the mirror!'

But when I looked into the mirror I cried out, and my heart was shaken; for I did not see myself there, but a devil's grimace and scornful laughter.

Indeed, all too well I understand the dream's sign and warning: my *teaching* is in danger, weeds want to be wheat!

My enemies have become powerful and have distorted the image of my teaching, so that those dearest to me must be ashamed of the gifts I gave them. (KSA, IV, 105–6)[2]

Since his new retreat, Zarathustra has understood the risk his giving runs both for him and for those who receive it, but his wisdom continues to grow and he can do nothing other than give. Strong in this further knowledge, in this confirmation obtained from his new solitude, Zarathustra can/must again descend among men, among his 'friends', to whom he has already given, but also among his 'enemies', who rejected that gift. Zarathustra's love, after this new retreat, knows no distinction: 'How I love everyone now, with whom I may simply speak! Even my enemies belong to my bliss.'[3] In this crucial passage from *Zarathustra*, the gift of wisdom finds its direction precisely in the love that overcomes all divisions and yet expresses the tension to the Over-man: 'Truly, there is a lake in me, a hermit-like and self-sufficient lake; but my torrent of love tears it along – down to the sea!'[4] The river of love that is the essence of accumulated wisdom does not permit Zarathustra his isolation, and urges him to establish relationships of 'friendship', so that he can communicate and give that wisdom so that the latter in the end leads to the Over-man, in the open sea, in whose continuous becoming every difference is overcome.

Zarathustra is therefore definitively forced to *empty himself* of this thought and to communicate it in the form of a gift to men, or rather to those who have ears for such wisdom. As the subtitle reminds us, *Thus Spoke Zarathustra* is '*ein Buch für Alle und Keine*' – a book for all and for none. It is not simply a subtitle whose meaning can be reduced – we would say today – to 'commercial' explanations, which, on the one hand, defining it a book 'for all', affirms its simplicity, its accessibility, and on the other hand, defining it a book 'for none' actually exerts a seduction and a flattery towards those who feel ready to decipher the enigma that it brings with it and to prove the author himself wrong on the alleged inaccessibility of the content. The subtitle should be read, rather, in light of the act of giving that Nietzsche intends to have carried out by writing *Zarathustra* – as has been said, he believes that he has given mankind 'the greatest gift' it has ever received and that he has written a 'sacred book' (the 'fifth Gospel', to be precise) with which he intends to challenge all other religions. In this sense, *Thus Spoke Zarathustra* is understood as 'a book for all and for none': it is in fact a book 'for all', since all are potential donees, all are in fact able to accept the gift that Zarathustra has in store for them, since all are granted access to the bottom of their soul at which *Zarathustra* is primarily directed in order to 'convert'⁵ man in the direction of the Over-man. Yet few understand the power of that gift, few can grasp its hidden meaning; and certainly 'none' can bring it to fruition: 'none', as the subtitle says (*ein Buch für Keine*), because whoever accepts it completely, must accept his own end, his own decline, since only from that decline can the Over-man be born.

The concept of the gift that Nietzsche uses in *Zarathustra* escapes to some extent from the dynamics and implications that are typically inherent in the gift and that we revisited earlier.⁶ However, Nietzsche consciously uses the device that the gift introduces into relationships – by establishing, altering or consolidating them – in order to clarify the unsettling nature of his message and to place it firmly within a precise tradition marked by the love of the Gospels as its desirable outcome.

With respect to the dynamics that are generally repeated in the gift, in *Zarathustra* a particular gift comes to light that feeds on itself and does not claim to derive 'value' from the donor, nor from the relationship within which the gift is realised or consolidated. The subject of the gift is here the gift itself: that is, the wisdom that wants to become a gift and that acts directly on the essence of both the donor and the person who receives or rejects that gift. The knowledge that Zarathustra possesses, following his isolation, modifies and constitutes Zarathustra himself, who in fact descends from the mountain as a *transformed being.* Here it is not at all the donor who constitutes the essence of the donated thing through his own will to power, it is certainly not Zarathustra who 'gives meaning' to the thing to be gifted, who *gives it intention*, who exerts that influence that charges it with the 'force' that it exerts on the donee, but rather the gift itself that acts on the donor and on the donee, determining them – both – in their essence and therefore in their relationship. In this consists the real overturning of the dynamics of giving introduced by Zarathustra: the subject of the gift is no longer a donor God that is distant and other from the men to whom he gives; the subject of the gift becomes the gift itself, to which is attributed an internal dynamics (in itself independent from donor and donee) and an autonomous force, which is immediately and spontaneously connected with the *Wille zur Macht*, and which completely affirms itself, in its extreme 'command', as 'will to love'.[7]

If God gives mankind creation and his Son in a relationship of *agape* love that he establishes and intends to see perpetuated by men in an ever insufficient imitation of that love (for God and between men through love of the neighbour), then with Zarathustra's gift it is love itself – as the ultimate and extreme 'command' law of the *Wille zur Macht* and as the universal bond that holds the All together – that expresses the dynamics and strength inherent in the gift. Each dispersed fragment therefore assumes its own independent value, independent of the relationship with a creator, and each individual acquires his own dignity as part of a totality to which he has always been connected. The gift of wisdom uses Zarathustra to reach the depths of men's souls and aims to awaken that dynamics that is sleepy and saturated in the isolation produced by that separation between the real world and the apparent world, which has ended up making everything insignificant in itself because it is somehow distinct from the always becoming totality. The gift therefore aims to awaken the will to power from its Apollonian 'crystallization' – which by now has exhausted its strength and its hold – and to turn it in the direction of the 'Dionysian', assigning to the resulting excess a precise aim marked by love for the Over-man: the new sense to be assigned to the earth (*der Sinn der Erde*).

If, as we have said, the subject of the relationship here is the gift itself, we must dwell on the nature of the Zarathustra as 'donor' used by Nietzsche and therefore of the donees who receive that gift from his hands.

Originally, Nietzsche planned for Zarathustra himself to announce the 'death of God' already in *The Gay Science*. However, he was convinced that it was more appropriate to reserve this first announcement for the *madman*, who is probably a reference to the historical figure of the cynical philosopher, follower of Antisthenes, Diogenes of Sinope, who lived in the fourth century BC. To him is assigned the task of announcing in the market square a truth that everyone knows and for which, however, no one has ears. Unlike Zarathustra, he does not bring new values, he does not bring with him a wisdom capable of overcoming that abyss opened by the 'death of God', his lantern has too weak a light and is lost 'in the clear light of the morning', that is, in the first rising of the 'morning philosophy' which for Nietzsche expresses the era in which free spirits have reached the freedom of reason and, having overcome the mists of metaphysics, are ready for a new dawn. However, the path that leads to the overcoming of God, understood as a stable foundation on which to set up one's own existence, is still a long one and the illusion of overcoming is easily transformed into the replacement of the old idol with new hypostasis and new certainties to idolize. The feeble light that the *madman* has in his lantern weakly announces the rising of a new sun – that wisdom that will later be brought as a gift from Zarathustra –, and it is necessarily lost in the morning light that advances on the market square.[8] The market is the place where the right value is assigned to and recognized in things, it is above all the place of exchange, and metaphorically expresses man's faith in terms of 'value' and in the idea that the 'values' that die can simply be replaced by others more capable and more resistant to time.[9] But it is no coincidence that the *madman*-Diogenes does not bring with him new values: his task is first of all to show the falsity of 'valorization' itself and the need for a 'transvaluation of all values', which is not simply the overcoming and replacement of the values that disappear with new and more effective ones, but the unmasking of the 'values' themselves and the insignificance on upon which they are based. If God dies, the expectation from which comes the possibility of valorization, understood as the recognition of an absolute 'value' (God, in fact) from which everything descends, is lost; understanding the death of God means recognizing in the assignment of 'value' a simply human exercise that cannot be banally resolved from the point of view of the exchange and replacement of old values with new ones, but rather requires a new wisdom still to come.

The choice of the *madman*-Diogenes for this first announcement that prepares the ground for the next messenger, Zarathustra, tells us a lot about Nietzsche's progress. That of the *madman* is a proper announcement, which has not yet taken on the character of a gift; of course, the image of the lantern alludes to a new 'light', but it is still a long way off and we still do not know the way through which it will reach men, if it will ever reach them capable of truly illuminating the way. It is for this reason that for this first step, rather than Zarathustra, Nietzsche preferred the figure of the *madman,* who is an explicit reference to Diogenes, the thinker who proposed the abolition of the social norms in force and the values underlying them and, recalling a total indifference (*adiaphora*) with respect to exteriority, hoped for a 'return to nature'. The *madman* has the task of announcing the 'death of God' and the consequent end of the 'values' that feed on that metaphysical foundation, but he does not have the task of proposing new 'values': his 'madness' testifies to the impossibility of communicating and of being listened to. He prepares the ground for Zarathustra's message, who is taking that 'decisive step' by integrating the announcement of the 'death of God' with a wisdom aimed at overcoming the abyss that the 'death of God' has opened wide. But for the new wisdom to take root it must be given, not taught or simply communicated, because in the latter form it would not respect the 'transvaluation of all values' that becomes necessary after the 'death of God' and would still respond to the dynamics of exchange, of substitution, of reward that the market effectively manifests both in *The Gay Science* and in *Thus Spoke Zarathustra*. The first announcement of the *madman* signals the impossibility of understanding the disturbing and revolutionary scope of the 'death of God' in a perspective of simple exchange and replacement of the old values with new ones, but it is the subsequent intervention of Zarathustra, who explicitly affirms that he has a 'gift' for men and that he is moved in his donation by a 'love' that has no limits or reason, that definitively clarifies the meaning of the 'transvaluation' and the dynamics that must now, after the 'death of God', be activated. 'Zarathustra's gift' is a sort of 'third paradigm' of the 'valorization', which takes over after the 'metaphysical paradigm', which assigns value from a divine source, and after the 'paradigm of the last man', which considers that one can overcome the metaphysical 'valorization' simply by assuming on oneself, on one's individuality, the complete responsibility of 'value'. In this way, what has an exchange 'value' is what ends up 'being of value' for man and the market repays to perfection this form of 'valorization' against which the paradigm of gift proposed by Zarathustra instead directs, where value no longer refers to anything else, but rather depends on the giving itself.

The gift takes over when Zarathustra perceives that the 'death of God' and the end of the metaphysical paradigm lead to the attribution of the declined value to the (last) man who lived and prospered in that metaphysical separation: the individual assumes upon himself the value that he had assigned to God and realizes a strengthening of the subject that in the end does nothing but overturn the metaphysical paradigm without, however, overcoming it, so that the same relationships within which these presumed new 'values' are determined are chosen by the logic of profit and the advantage for the subject. Against this 'economic' vision of 'valorization', with its gift of wisdom and love, Zarathustra intends to suggest a full 'transvaluation of all values', a new paradigm for the attribution of 'value', which goes beyond good and evil or rather a logic that gives value according to what is good or evil *for* the person involved in the relationship. By echoing the love of the Gospels and the gratuitousness that goes with it, Zarathustra shows the possibility of continuing that love beyond the metaphysical separation between the real world and the apparent world, and its constant – and at times violent – attack on Christianity, its values and its shifts, is but an attempt to recover what of that tradition must be preserved and continued after the 'death of God'. The possibility of this 'transvaluation' passes through a clear gap that Zarathustra's gift presents with respect to the dynamics that can usually be reconstructed in the donation.

As said, here the subject of the gift, what gives value and establishes the relationships within which the donation happens, is not the donor nor the donee but the gift itself. The value is not assigned starting from the exchange that takes place, that is, starting from the will to power of the donor nor from the response of the donee, since it is the gift itself that has 'value' beyond what is good and bad for the donor and for the one who receives (or rejects) it. Here a reference to gold also takes on a particular meaning, a metal that always gives itself and that has its own value within itself, because it is of value without reference to anything else that might give it value.[10] With the 'death of God' the (metaphysical) instance from which the 'value' is assigned disappears, and only what in and of itself is 'of value' is revealed as having 'value'. 'The highest values devalue themselves, the aim is lacking, and "why" finds no answer' (KSA, XII, 350) can be read in an 1887 aphorism (9 [35]), but the picture is already clear in a passage of the 1873 book *On Truth and Lies in a Nonmoral Sense*:

> What then is truth? A movable host of metaphors, metonymies, and; anthropomorphisms: in short, a sum of human relations which have been poetically and rhetorically intensified, transferred, and embellished, and which, after long usage, seem to a people to be fixed, canonical, and binding. Truths are illusions which we have forgotten are illusions – they are metaphors that have become worn out and have been drained of sensuous

force, coins which have lost their embossing and are now considered as metal and no longer as coins. (KSA, I, 880–1)[11]

When the metaphysical value of the coin disappears, what remains is the intrinsic value of the metal of which the coin is made. However, if this value is assigned only through the exchange, and therefore from a 'valorization' still linked to man as the yardstick of valorization, the reference to gold, a metal that always gives itself due to its innumerable merits and that seems to escape at least partially from the dynamics of mere exchange, is a reference to the 'gift' as a possible way for the new 'valorization' that is carried out as the realization of accomplished or active nihilism.[12]

After the metaphysical 'valorization', Zarathustra's gift proposes a new form of 'valorization':[13] what is of value, what has value, is here the gift itself which in its necessary dynamics (there is no gift outside the act of giving) transfers 'value' to those who receive it and to those who in turn bear it. Zarathustra is therefore not to be considered outside the gift with which he is charged and as a result of which he is now a 'transformed'. The historical figure of Zarathustra derives 'value' precisely and only by virtue of the gift he has received and which he is now ready to give in his turn. Certainly, just as happens inversely in the classical dynamics that describes the gift in which the value in itself of the donated object is not immaterial, but derives its definitive 'value' from the combination of its (presumed) intrinsic value with the will to power of the donor in relation to (relationship with) the donee, in a similar way here the donee/donor Zarathustra should not be attributed his 'value' exclusively from his historical figure, even if evidently this cannot be immaterial to the role assigned to him and which he constantly keeps to. The authentic 'value' comes from the gift itself, from that particular subject of the gift that is the *Wille zur Macht*, and yet the choice of Zarathustra as the bearer of the gift and mediator among men to whom he in turn gives is by no means trivial. 'I have not been asked, as I should have been asked, what the name of Zarathustra means to me, in my capacity as the first immoralist' (KSA, VI, 367),[14] observes

Nietzsche in *Ecce Homo*, urging an investigation that will reveal the meaning of his choice. In Nietzsche's eyes, Zarathustra[15] is the founder of morality, and he must therefore also be the first to *recognize* that error in order to overcome it: from the point of view of a transvaluation of all values, the genealogical recourse to Zarathustra is functional to the unmasking of their groundlessness, but it is also functional to the 'position' of new values that are so manifestly unfounded. But it is precisely from that groundlessness that they derive their 'strength', which resides entirely in the tension towards the Over-man, in the love that knows no distinctions and that freely orients the will to power in its unexhausted becoming.

Nietzsche's prophet Zarathustra does not correspond at all with the Persian prophet: what he teaches and professes in the pages of Nietzsche's work has little or nothing to do with the content of his historical doctrine. Rather, he drew from his long isolation from men a wisdom of which he was unaware and which 'transformed' him, making him now the ideal messenger for the overcoming of morality and the advent of the Over-man. Born according to some in 588 BC and to others in 630 BC, the historical figure Zarathustra was the founder of a sort of dualism between Good and Evil, represented by the opposition between the god Ohrmazd, lord of light, and the god Ahriman, lord of darkness. The contrast described by Zarathustra did not, however, present itself as a distinction that would discredit the matter in favour of the spiritual realm. Indeed, his doctrine attributed great value and dignity to the *body*, and in this it certainly presents a point of contact with Nietzsche's philosophy, which in fact speaks of the great reason of the body, distinguishing it from the small reason of the spirit.[16] It has also been observed that Zoroastrianism and Nietzschean thought also converge on other points such as the complementarity between good and evil, the critique of the concept and practice of revenge, and the objection to the tyranny of the past and future over the present. But beyond some theoretical affinities, which do exist, the choice of an Oriental as an indicator of the philosophical and cultural destiny of the West is probably intended to underline the peculiarity of its message and its sapiential character. There is in fact no logical argument behind the doctrine of Zarathustra, rather it has the character of a wisdom of life that takes over to determine and suggest a particular *Weltanschauung*. Nietzsche uses Zarathustra to let the dynamics of the gift of wisdom act in the most effective way, which he intends to activate as a mechanism for unmasking the falsehood of values and for overcoming the nihilistic-passive drift in the 'position' of new values that orient man towards the Over-man. The choice of the original donee who must in turn become a donor falls on the prophet Zarathustra, who, 'transformed' by his wisdom, is forced by he himself to empty himself in order to communicate that knowledge to men. This is where the dynamics of the gift finally come into play, which Nietzsche intends to use as a narrative and argumentative device. Although the actual donor is not Zarathustra, once he has come down from his mountain, it is in this capacity that he presents himself to those he meets, and it is always to him – as a donor – that the answer, whether positive or negative, to the gift seems to be directed. Travel companions, friends, guests are presented in this particular 'relationship' with the donor Zarathustra, but this is only an illusion, since from the very first lines of the prologue the reader knows that he is nothing but a mediator who will necessarily have to be forgotten, just as the book he has in his hands will have to be abandoned once he has understood it and accepted its message, since it (like Zarathustra himself) is nothing more than a tool for overcoming. In fact, the gift that Zarathustra brings with him also implies the renunciation of the bond with 'Zarathustra the donor', since the latter performs a simple function of service to the gift itself,[17] that is, to the will to power, which is the authentic donor subject.

Like a river that makes its way through the obstacles on the ground to flow into the sea, so the wisdom that overflows from Zarathustra (from the lake of his solitude) seeks its way among men to reach the Over-man and in its passage can only transform what it meets into the means necessary to achieve its end. The 'value' of men lies in the function they are willing to perform, that is, in their ability to make the advent of the *Übermensch* possible: 'What is great about human beings is that they are a bridge and not a purpose: what is lovable about human beings is that they are a *crossing over* [*Übergang*] and a *going under* [*Untergang*]' (KSA, IV, 16–17).[18]

What Zarathustra is looking for is in fact 'donees' who know how to fully accept the gift of wisdom that he is offering them and who therefore know how to become a 'bridge' for the Over-man and know how to destine themselves to their own decline by renouncing themselves. The gift of wisdom that Zarathustra carries with him presents its own danger from the 'Prologue' onwards. Every gift is poisonous, every gift conceals a danger in itself, and Zarathustra's gift is certainly no exception to this rule. 'A golden sun and around it the snake of knowledge!' this is perhaps the most significant image of Zarathustra's gift: an overflowing wealth that turns out to be a poisonous,[19] lethal wisdom for those who receive it. In bringing 'his' deadly gift to men, Zarathustra is, however, accompanied by his animals, the eagle and the snake, which respectively represent the *pride* of a wisdom that makes all other knowledge vain and sterile in comparison and the (poisonous) *cunning* with which such wisdom must creep into the ears of men so that they may listen to it and in the end die *for* it, so that from their decline the Over-man may be born. Pride and poisonous cunning compete to seduce and ensnare the donees that Zarathustra is looking for in order to launch them into their decline ('*mein Gang ist ihr Untergang*') in the name of love for the Over-man. But his search is not at all easy and the ploy of the gift (which in itself contains the *pride* of the wealth that is promised and the *cunning* that hides the poisonous nature of wisdom) is delegated to 'select' those who can receive it and follow its destiny.

We know that Nietzsche draws his sources about the gift mainly from classical and Nordic mythology, without of course ignoring the Holy Scriptures. In the *Edda*, for example, a mythological saga that Nietzsche read and re-read in his early years and which constituted a constant cultural basis for his entire speculative range, the gift is presented as a sacred necessity, a moral and juridical duty that one is obliged to observe, but which always carries within itself a danger. As can be seen from a passage in *Havamal*, one of the old poems of the *Edda* which in 1922 Mauss used as an epigraph in his *Essay on the Gift*, this mythological saga explicitly warns against the extreme risk involved in the gift:

It is better not to beg [ask for something]
Than to sacrifice too much [to the gods]:
A present given always expects one in return.
It is better not to bring any offering
Than to spend too much on it.

Using the ploy of the gift, Nietzsche certainly knows that he is recalling the compensatory dynamics we have been discussing, but he also knows that he is using a complex and articulated mechanism that acts on different levels and at different intensities. In fact, it is possible to identify an initial *religious* level of the gift, which is expressed in the form of sacrifice, or of homage to the divinity; a second *economic*, so to speak, level linked to exchange and reward; and a third *juridical* level, in which the gift takes the form of ransom, of payment imposed as a consequence of a crime to be redeemed. Aware of the many meanings that the act of giving brings with it, in presenting Zarathustra's message as a 'gift', Nietzsche activates all three levels of giving through a general rethinking of the first and most relevant of the meanings inherent in giving, the 'religious' one.[20] It is also in this sense that the 'selection' and role of the 'donees', who receive the poisonous gift by accepting their 'sacrifice' – which is also the 'sacrifice' of an overall conception of 'value' linked to the acquisition, exchange and reward distinctive of the economic level of the gift, as well as the conception of 'responsibility', guilt, and reparation linked to the 'legal' (and ethical) level of the gift – should be thought. The wisdom of Zarathustra once accepted, with the 'sacrifice' that it demands of those who fully accept, restores to the gift its innocence and liberates it from the old religious, economic and juridical conceptions of the gift, which dies at once with the 'death of God'. In short, Zarathustra's gift makes use of the classical dynamics of donation to 'pass' from donor to donee and communicate its content of wisdom. Such wisdom, however, once fully accepted, reveals the excess of Zarathustra's gift with respect to those dynamics, and this excess resides precisely in the 'will to love' that commands the donation.

The poisonous component that constantly accompanies the seductive aspect of Zarathustra's gift is simply functional to the extinction of such fundamental characteristics: Zarathustra's gift reveals the perverse dynamics of the gift by making use of it, but it is the overcoming of them at the end that it aims to achieve, that is, the Beyond man. It is wrong to think that giving-squandering is functional to itself; in fact, from this point of view one cannot understand the tension to the *Übermensch*, nor can one understand the continuous and arduous search for donees, who in this perspective would turn out to be mere replicants of Zarathustra. Not giving in itself, as a wasting and squandering of energy, but giving as a gift of love and wisdom is the nerve centre of *Zarathustra*, as the 'greatest gift' ever offered to humanity and above all as the 'fifth Gospel'. The donees Zarathustra is looking for must in turn be prepared to become donors themselves of this wisdom in a relationship of love for the whole, which is hidden in the depths of the soul, and which inexorably condemns them to the decline of their own individuality matured in the oblivion of that common belonging. If Zarathustra has obtained that wisdom in his solitude, now he seeks to awaken that wisdom in those who are willing to follow him in his preaching. Even if at first he thinks he can find a listening audience in the crowd gathered at the market, he very quickly understands that there he will not find those who are ready to follow him, nor will he find beneficiaries authentically capable of 'responding' to the gift, without turning his wisdom into a doctrine to follow.

> It dawned on me: I need companions, and living ones – not dead companions
> and corpses that I carry with me wherever I want.

Instead I need living companions who follow me because they want to follow themselves – wherever I want.

It dawned on me: let Zarathustra speak not to the people, but instead to companions! Zarathustra should not become the shepherd and dog of a herd! (KSA, IV, 25)[21]

Zarathustra knows that his gift can find beneficiaries only in those who feel in themselves (in the depths of their soul) the common will that animates Zarathustra and choose to follow him because ultimately, they are simply following their own will. Zarathustra speaks of travel companions, of *Gefährten*, because they are willing to proceed on the same path that destiny has marked for Zarathustra, that decline from which the new dawn of the Over-man will be born. Zarathustra's path (*Gang*), joined by his companions, coincides with his and their decline *(Unter-gang)*. Like Zarathustra, they accept the wisdom that now shines in them in order to give themselves and communicate to others ready to accept it.

Whoever receives Zarathustra's gift becomes rich with his own light, not because of a simple transfer of energy, but rather because he finds in himself that richness that he had forgotten. The reference to the sun mentioned above should not be read as a transfer of energy that comes to Zarathustra from his solitude and then passes to his donees. Rather, it is a gift that reactivates the dormant energy and awakens the richness present in each person: that is, their original co-belonging to the All. This becomes particularly clear in the speech 'The Night Song'.

It is night: only now all the songs of the lovers awaken. And my soul too is the song of a lover.

An unstilled, an unstillable something is in me; it wants to be heard. A craving for love is in me, which itself speaks the language of love.

I am light; oh that I were night! But this is my loneliness, that I am girded by light [. . .]

But I live in my own light, I drink back into myself the flames that break out of me.

I do not the know the happiness of receiving; and often I dreamed that stealing must be more blessed than receiving.

This is my poverty, that my hand never rests from bestowing; this is my envy, that I see waiting eyes and the illuminated nights of longing.

Oh misery of all bestowers! [. . .]

They receive from me, but do I still touch their souls? There is a cleft between giving and receiving; and the closest cleft is the last to be bridged. (KSA, IV, 136–7)[22]

This passage from *Zarathustra* can only be understood because one can see the desperation that pervades the donor. It is in the night that Zarathustra's light shines and highlights his loneliness; if during the day 'his' light is confused and lost in the sunlight, then in the night it stands out and reveals his loneliness and strength, which are the loneliness and strength of those who know how to receive his gift and awaken that light of their own hidden in the depths of their soul. To reach it, it is necessary to become a donor in the same way as Zarathustra, who gives everything and keeps nothing for himself, but occupying this position of bestowers *sans emploi*, of mere donors, creates further separations and increases the loneliness, as well as the nastiness that lurks in it:

A hunger grows out of my beauty; I wish to harm those for whom I shine, I wish to rob those on whom I have bestowed: – thus I hunger for malice [. . .]

My happiness in bestowing died in bestowing, my virtue wearied of itself in its superabundance! For one who always bestows, the danger is loss of shame; whoever dispenses always has calloused hands and heart from sheer dispensing. (KSA, IV, 137)[23]

Zarathustra's giving-squandering requires a law of love to discipline and guide him, and this law has its roots in the depths of the soul which Zarathustra now despairs of having 'touched' with his giving. Zarathustra's continuous giving does not become realised in itself in a sort of philosophy of *dépense* that in a form of *potlatch* activates a virtuous circle capable of overcoming the economic dynamics of 'value'. The 'desperation' of his loneliness is a further revealing sign of the need to overcome this form of donation as well. Zarathustra's giving always runs the risk of being misunderstood, and the desperation of his loneliness is always there to signal that risk. Loneliness is never the end, it is simply a means of acquiring the right distance from the crowd, it is not a landing place, as, rather, it always ends up distorting the sense of isolation in an illusory strengthening of self.

The neighbour and the friend

His lightness and joy are manifested instead when the giving is aimed at his own extinction in the tension to the Over-man, who genuinely knows no loneliness or distinctions of any kind. In the common tension to the Over-man, to whom he exhorts, Zarathustra finds the authentic meaning of his gift, and the desperation of his loneliness is overcome by the bond of *friendship* that binds him to his donees, whose soul he has truly touched. It is ultimately *friends* that Zarathustra needs in order to give his wisdom, because a friend is the one who finds at the bottom of his soul the same tension to overcome and wants with a single will. But the friend is by no means a safe port in which to berth, he is rather the one who challenges and endangers his own certainties and threatens autocratic solitude:

> 'Onc is always too many around me' – thus thinks the hermit. 'Always one times one – in the long run that makes two!' I and me are always too eager in conversation: how could I stand it if there were no friend?
>
> For the hermit the friend is always a third: the third is the cork that prevents the conversation of the two from sinking into the depths. (KSA, IV, 71)[24]

The friend saves the hermit from loneliness (the one who lives on his own loneliness), but at the same time puts his certainties at risk, spurs him on, challenges him; in this 'dangerous' relationship that is friendship, Nietzsche sees the resource capable of allowing the 'passage' of Zarathustra's gift: it is precisely in friendship that the love relationship to be reactivated and which is capable of orienting towards the Over-man lies. Zarathustra does not need disciples, but friends to whom he can communicate his 'horizontal' love, which has abandoned all recourse to transcendence and 'vertical' relationships. In the master-disciple relationship a disparity is preserved that Zarathustra aims to overcome; the very origin of wisdom prevents such a hierarchy. Friendship, on the other hand, immediately creates an equal footing, an equal level of sharing, of common belonging and common destiny. And with the figure of the friend, Nietzsche intends in particular to 'correct' the love for one's neighbour. In Nietzsche's intentions, in fact, the description of the recipient of the love and wisdom that Zarathustra brings as a gift must further confirm the 'perfecting' of the 'good news' that he intends to bring to completion with his 'fifth-Gospel'. In the passage from love of one's neighbour to love of one's friend, it becomes clear, however, that the movement put in place by Nietzsche cannot in any way be thought of as an elimination of Christianity as a doctrine considered insignificant and useless, but rather as an attempt to take up and 'continue' a doctrine corrupted by misunderstandings and simplifications functional to the will to overwhelm. In fact, love of the friend does not substitute the love of one's neighbour: strictly speaking, love of the friend is a simple revival of that ultimate 'commandment' that is fulfilled for Nietzsche only beyond the separation between the real world and the apparent world. By overcoming the love of one's neighbour, Nietzsche intends to overcome the compassionate love that 'nails' the beloved object and prevents its freedom. But the compassionate love he rails against is, for Nietzsche, nothing other than the outcome of a misunderstood and betrayed doctrine, which must instead be salvaged in its deepest tension.

Woe to all lovers who do not yet have an elevation that is above their pitying!

[. . .] all great love is above even all its pitying, for it still wants to create the beloved!

'I offer myself to my love, and my neighbour as myself' – thus it is said of all creators. (KSA, IV, 115–16)[25]

While pitying (literally) 'nails' the beloved object, Zarathustra in his infinite love (re)creates the object to be loved, and in the friend to whom he gives he awakens in the depths of his soul that same love that he wants to create and wants to *give meaning to* in a world that he has discovered to be meaningless. For this love, which is the will to create, it is necessary to sacrifice oneself, and with oneself it is necessary to sacrifice every love that preserves and keeps the beloved object – that is the 'neighbour' in the sense misunderstood and criticized by Nietzsche – inert in the pitying.

> You creators, you higher men! One is pregnant only with one's own child. Do not let yourselves be misled and spoon-fed! Who after all is your neighbour? And even if you act 'for your neighbour' – still you don't create for him! Unlearn this 'for', you creators; your virtue itself wants that you do nothing 'for' and 'in order' and 'because.'
>
> You should plug your ears against these false little words.
>
> 'For your neighbour' is the virtue of only small people; there they say 'birds of a feather' and 'one hand washes the other' – they have neither the right nor the strength to your self-interest. In your self-interest, you creators, are the precaution and providence of the pregnant! What no one yet has laid eyes on, the fruit: your whole love shelters and spares and nourishes it.
>
> Where your whole love is, with your children, there too your whole virtue is! Your work, your will is your 'neighbour' – do not let yourself be spoon-fed any false values! (KSA, IV, 362)[26]

The image of the 'neighbour' against whom Nietzsche rails, is the image produced by the general misunderstanding of the *agape* bond to which this love refers. Love of one's neighbour derives strictly from the love of God and for God; in Luke we read: "'Love the Lord your God with all your heart and with all your soul and with all your strength and with all your mind"; and,

"Love your neighbour as yourself"' (Lk. 10.27),[27] the same love (*agapán*) that
is directed to God must be directed to one's neighbour, but the relationship of
love between men as the highest commandment does not taper into a generic
love for God,[28] in an attempt to reciprocate that love that is always doomed
to failure.[29] Nietzsche intends to overcome love of the neighbour because his
primary objective is to overcome the break between the ideal world and the
apparent world, but he recognizes in that love for the neighbour a value that
in fact transfers into love for the friend. Already in *agape* any compensatory-
rewarding schema seems to fail in the face of the commandment of love of
one's neighbour,[30] however, according to Nietzsche, such love is prevented in
its effects by the original lie that separates God from man and creation. The
'new' love that he professes in partial continuity with the love of the Gospels
is aimed at this. From the 'neighbour', therefore, too tied to the God that hides
behind him, to the 'friend' who has no metaphysical coating to refer to, but
only a common origin and a possible common tension. In the transition from
love of one's neighbour to love of one's friend, Nietzsche intends to overcome
the misunderstanding that sees in the love of one's neighbour a compassionate
love but, as was rightly observed by Massimo Cacciari, it is precisely in the love
of the friend professed by Zarathustra that

> we find the *liberating* traits of closeness. The relationship of *philia* is not
> fulfilled if it does not keep within itself, in all their drama, the traits of the
> *plesios*. The relationship with the friend is inseparable from the relationship
> with that abyssally remote neighbour that the ego discovers to be for itself,
> as soon as it begins the ascent from its cave.[31]

When Nietzsche, through Zarathustra, exhorts us to move from love of one's
neighbour to love of the remote, of the future, he is in fact reaffirming what is
already contained in the commandment of love one's neighbour, that is, love
for those who are most distant, remote, for the unfamiliarity that the other
– who, in fact, approaches us – always holds.[32] As said, Nietzsche intends to

overcome the misunderstood figure of the neighbour through the love of the friend, but here we find the fundamental traits of that figure and of that dramatic 'commandment' that imposes love for the stranger on us, love for what perturbs and puts at risk our 'loneliness', our 'blessed island': exactly what is prescribed for love of the friend/enemy.

> You cannot stand yourselves and do not love yourselves enough: now you want to seduce your neighbour to love and gild yourselves with his error [. . .]
>
> One person goes to his neighbour because he seeks himself, and the other because he would like to lose himself. Your bad love of yourselves makes your loneliness into a prison. (KSA, IV, 78)[33]

The gift is always potentially pregnant with evil consequences,[34] Zarathustra continually reveals this in his search for donees, the danger is always lurking. The wisdom he brings as a gift is poisonous, but Zarathustra cannot refrain from giving; this is his loneliness and his condemnation, from which he can free himself only by emptying himself of that wisdom among those who know how to listen and – like him – to definitively decline for it. Zarathustra knows that the gift must be overcome, but he is aware of his 'condemnation': 'I, however, am a bestower. Gladly I bestow as friend to friends', because in this relationship of friendship it is as if the gift is overcome and loses the most pernicious dynamics that accompany it. A passage by Emerson, an important and constant source for Nietzsche, shows how it is possible to overcome the violent and overwhelming dynamics inherent in the gift in a relationship of love.

> The law of benefits is a difficult channel, which requires careful sailing, or rude boats. It is not the office of a man to receive gifts. How dare you give them? We wish to be self-sustained. We do not quite forgive a giver. The hand that feeds us is in some danger of being bitten. We can receive anything from love, for that is a way of receiving it from ourselves; but not from anyone who assumes to bestow.[35]

In the essay 'On Gifts and Presents', Emerson reveals that in love only a gift that does not bring resentment and obligation is possible. Only from love can we receive, because it is like receiving from ourselves. When Nietzsche alludes to the gift 'from friend to friend', he is most likely thinking of this very type of gift, in which the donor is love itself, which *passes* from friend to friend, strengthening the relationship of friendship (*philia*), the bond that binds friends in their common origin and common tension. '[T]hat is a way of receiving it from ourselves; but not from anyone who assumes to bestow,' writes Emerson, and the dynamics seems to be repeated in Zarathustra's gift, which *passes* from 'friend' to 'friend' the very love he has found in the depths of his soul, in his loneliness. Zarathustra gives nothing in itself but a 'wisdom' capable of awakening in those who know how to listen to it that light that lies dormant and forgotten at the ground of the soul; once it is reactivated, it is capable of restitching that (now) frayed bond with the All. As said, that light can again blur or, worse, get lost in the arrogant solitude of the presumed 'chosen', that is to say, it can always turn again to love for the 'friend' that in the end leads to the tension to the Over-man, to the common desire to give up one's individuality in that rediscovered light.

> I do not teach you the neighbour, but the friend [. . .]. I teach you the friend in whom the world stands complete, a bowl of goodness – the creating friend who always has a complete world to bestow. [. . .] Let the future and the farthest be the cause of your today: in your friend you shall love the overman as your cause. (KSA, IV, 78)[36]

The love for the friend contains the tension to the *adveniens*, but above all it contains the reference to a common root. In the friend, who is also and above all an enemy[37] because he challenges us and puts our stability at risk, lies the possibility to get out of our 'loneliness' and the risk that it brings with it; the relationship with the friend allows us to find in ourselves that same wealth that the friend constitutes for us: through the friend we get out of the sterile I-Me relationship, we overcome the spirit of gravity that immobilizes and sterilizes the bottom of our soul and we can free our will in the direction of the Over-man.

In the friend one must be able to find that 'nobility'[38] of which one is capable and which makes possible the openness to the coming of the Over-man. In this the friend/enemy is the closest to us, he is the obstacle that reveals, in the confrontation that saves from loneliness as an end in itself, the bottom of our own soul to us, a co-belonging that frees us to a common (possible and, therefore, free) tension, that is the love for the *Übermensch*.

In his friend, Zarathustra loves the one who knows how to renounce himself in order to give himself to the Over-man, and in his friend he finds that love which is the same dynamics that animates his overflowing heart which cannot help but give itself. Zarathustra does not simply exhort a friend relationship between men, he himself needs friends so that the loneliness of his lake overflows into rivers that eventually lead to the sea of the Over-man. He himself needs to find donees if he does not want to drown his highest hope in the lake which he has built within himself. Every great loneliness runs this risk. It has been said, 'the friend [. . .] is the cork that prevents the conversation of the [I and me] from sinking into the depths', it is the pretext that restores solitude, though necessary as an isolation from the crowd trapped by the networks of metaphysics and clouded by the passive nihilistic decline, to a common belonging and a 'possible' common destiny of overcoming.

The friend is capable of showing this ability to separate from himself, to draw from the depths of the soul, which is by no means a deeper and more separated ego, but rather immediate contact with the All to which we have always belonged. The friend is the one who shows *us* the capacity of 'detachment' from oneself, the ability to break oneself in order to open up to the Over-man. But the friend is the other from me that I myself always am: with the passage from neighbour to friend, Zarathustra does not intend to select an elite, but to show how love so understood is capable of establishing relationships of friendship in the solitude.[39] Just as the neighbour does not identify a particular 'species' but simply the one who, from his extraneousness, approaches and imposes a response of love on us, in a similar way the friend should not be understood as a member of a special 'caste' of chosen ones ready to overcome: by loving the friend in the other, I simply dispose myself to 'detachment' and open myself to overcoming individuation.

Zarathustra's gift is a gift of love and wisdom, because in its giving itself it repeats the love that leads to the Over-man, whose wisdom is not a knowledge that comes from remote distances, but from the depths of the soul, as we read in some passages from part three of *Zarathustra*, certainly the most theoretically dense book of the four.

> Up, abysmal thought, out of my depths! I am your rooster and dawn. (KSA, IV, 270)[40]
>
> ---
>
> Oh my soul, I gave you back your freedom over what is created and uncreated: and who knows as you know the lust of future things? (KSA, IV, 278)[41]

In passages such as these, it becomes clear that the wisdom Zarathustra intends to give as a gift is nothing but the emergence of a knowledge present in each one in his own 'depths', hidden in the trade between men who have become a crowd and still misunderstood in their solitude, if this latter is simply intended as an end in itself. The virtue that it gives exhorts us to overcome the obstacles connected with solitude, which if on the one hand allow access to the depths of the soul, then on the other can sink into the most blind selfishness.

> That the solitary height not isolate and suffice itself eternally; that the mountain come to the valley and the winds of the height to the lowlands –
>
> Oh who would find the right christening and glistening name for such longing! 'Bestowing virtue' – thus Zarathustra once named the unnameable.
>
> And it was then that it happened – indeed happened for the first time! – that his words pronounced selfishness blessed, the sound, healthy selfishness that wells from a powerful soul. (KSA, IV, 238)[42]

With the expression 'bestowing virtue' Zarathustra tries to give a name to what cannot be defined by a name (the unnameable, *das Unnennbare*): with the 'bestowing virtue' Zarathustra describes a dynamics that must accompany the Over-man, but which in itself and for itself does not yet mean anything, and indeed always runs the risk of being misunderstood in the sense of the exaltation of selfishness, lust and the continuous affirmation of domination.

The three things defined as 'bad' by traditional morality – sensual pleasure, lust for domination and selfishness – find a new light in the *great noontide*, where selfishness no longer corresponds to the isolation and strengthening of the individual but constitutes the key to the Over-man's Openness. Like sensual pleasure and lust for domination, selfishness (the will to individuation and its strengthening) is always a danger to those who touch the bottom of their soul and it stops at that continuous squandering, without rather opening itself up to the *beyond-self* and correctly directing that flow that comes from the depths of its own soul.

Love your friend as you love yourself – one could say it paraphrasing the words of the Gospel, provided, however, that one understands that love in the new sense offered by Zarathustra, that is, as a willingness to overcome oneself in the will to create that leads to the Over-man. In this sense the friend is such precisely because through him we can see and share the wealth that unites us in the depths of our soul and not because in him resides an elective trait that we must emulate. In short, one cannot think that the friend immediately coincides with the 'higher man': the figure of the friend simply describes the love relationship that must be established/restored and then turned towards the Over-man.

This point is further clarified by the fourth part in *Zarathustra*. Entirely dedicated to the higher man and written by Nietzsche after the first three with which he had initially considered the work to be finished, this fourth part constitutes on several levels a real test of the conceptual tenacity of 'Zarathustra's gift' and its practical effectiveness.

4

About the new love

Tutti li miei penser parlan d'Amore

e ànno i·lloro sì gran varietate

ch'altro mi fa voler sua potestate,

altro folle ragiona il suo valore,

altro sperando m'aporta dolzore,

altro pianger mi fa spesse fïate,

e sol s'accordano in cherer pietate

tremando di paura, che è nel core.

Dante, *Vita nova* [1]

Hospitality

Through the 'honey sacrifice', Zarathustra draws the 'higher men' he has met on his preaching journey to his cave by offering them 'hospitality', a relationship intrinsically linked to the dynamics of giving. Zarathustra thinks he has identified possible donees in them – he certainly considers them worthy to receive the gift for which he came down from his mountain – but he seems doubtful about their ability to 'respond' adequately to the gift. By hosting them, he hopes to achieve the purpose inherent in his gift, but at the same time he is suspicious of their ability to fully accept the effects of the donation; his 'hospitality' thus becomes the ultimate test of their 'fidelity' to the wisdom he offers them. Their 'superiority' lies in sensing, albeit to varying degrees, the gravity of the moment humanity is going through in the era of 'the death of God', but Zarathustra has not yet identified 'friends' in them, in the above sense, and his objective is that the honey sacrifice as well as the outcome of the relationship of 'hospitality' will – or not – reveal their ability to be authentically *friends*, entering into the relationship of love for the all. And, in fact, the disappointment that Zarathustra will feel about their 'response' will reveal and confirm that his gift is not trivially aimed at 'chosen' people, but to all those who are genuinely ready to listen to the deepest voice of their soul, because the 'love of the *friend*', in the double meaning of the genitive, only renews the free love for oneself and for one's own belonging to the continuous becoming of the All.

In this fourth part dedicated to higher men, Nietzsche intends to show how the love of a friend always runs the risk of turning into 'compassion' for those higher men. The love to which Nietzsche exhorts through the figure of the friend, which replaces the (misunderstood) figure of the 'neighbour', aims to overcome every distinction and every privilege, and shows how even those who seem closer to the overcoming can in fact conceal the desire to preserve their subjectivity, the self-love that does not allow them to look beyond the I-Me relationship, and condemns them to sink into their individuality.

Through the 'honey sacrifice' Zarathustra draws the *höheren Menschen* (higher men) to him and, meeting them on his way, sends them to his cave where he offers them 'hospitality'. Both 'sacrifice' and 'hospitality' refer, as we know, to the broader concept of 'giving'. It almost seems as if in this fourth part we are witnessing a sort of Shakespearean 'mousetrap', or rather a staging aimed at revealing the reasons why Zarathustra used the 'gift' to communicate his message and how this dynamics contributes to overcoming it.

First, the 'sacrifice'. The book opens with Zarathustra again alone, sitting on a boulder in front of his cave. His wisdom and loneliness have further transformed him, the watery image of the lake that needs to overflow and become a river to flow into the open sea of the *Übermensch* is replaced by the image of the thickest honey that 'makes my blood thicker and also makes my soul calmer' (*KSA*, IV, 296),[2] in fact closing Zarathustra in his loneliness so he cannot communicate. It is at this point that Zarathustra thinks about the 'honey sacrifice', which is the sacrifice of his loneliness, that is, the will to 'make sacred' his own isolation by renouncing it. But it is not a true 'sacrifice': 'What sacrifice! I squander what was bestowed me, I the squanderer with a thousand hands: How could I call that – sacrificing!' The honey sacrifice turns out to be a further ploy used by Zarathustra to attract men and to be able to donate-communicate his wisdom. Almost as Lucretius uses poetry, the honey of muses, to communicate a doctrine that 'usually appears too severe to those who have not tried it',[3] so Zarathustra uses the honey 'sacrifice' to attract men as much with the sweetness that the 'honey' promises with its colour that is similar to the yellow of gold and the sun, as with the 'sacrifice' and what this religious practice evokes, but which here must find its definitive unmasking. Already in the expression 'honey sacrifice' squandering and spending are alluded to, and are always in reality included in 'sacrifice' in general;[4] in the sacrifice 'officiated' by Zarathustra this fundamental aspect becomes even more manifest, not at all to be hidden as a shameful mystery but rather to be exalted as an action to continue and 'sanctify'. The call to 'sacrifice' is to be read in a comparison with the 'sacrifice' of Jesus who descends among men and which culminates in the cross. This is confirmed by the reference shortly after to the 'golden fishing rod' with which Zarathustra wants to 'bait the oddest human fishes'[5] in a clear echo of the Gospel metaphor: 'I will send you out to fish for people' (Mt. 4.19), Jesus promises the humble fishermen he meets along the Sea of Galilee.[6] But it is also confirmed by the temptations that Zarathustra, like Jesus, is called to face and overcome. The first of these temptations, as we have said, is his own 'loneliness', which apparently satisfies him, but which he overcomes due to the compulsive need he has in himself to give and empty himself; the other is 'compassion', which harnesses the love to which he aspires by 'nailing' the beloved object. The entire fourth part is crisscrossed by this continuous low which is the desperate cry of the higher man invoking Zarathustra's compassionate help, constituting the last and greatest temptation that he is called to overcome to 'free' his love.

As mentioned, that the 'honey sacrifice' should be read in opposition to the 'sacrifice' of Jesus that Nietzsche stages to signal the 'leap' that must be made to move from compassionate love to the love of the Over-man, obviously does not mean that we should stop at the restoration of this dynamics of the *dépense* contained in the sacrifice of Zarathustra. This is because, on the one hand, such a dynamics simply aimed at excess and squandering is not in itself able to lead to the Over-man without the direction that only love can give[7] and, on the other, because the particular 'sacrifice' of Jesus, son of God, already 'unmasks' the mechanism behind the death of the perfect victim. Without necessarily having to disturb Girard[8] and his reflections on the victimization mechanism, the crucifixion as the sacrificial death of God himself has the potential within itself to reveal what is implicit in sacrifice – if only because in the crucifixion one claims to 'sacrifice' the Son of God, that is 'make sacred' in the process what is already necessarily so.

Having shown the dynamics of sacrifice and exalted the continuous donation in it devoted to continuous squandering and wasting, a further step is needed in the direction already marked by the love of Jesus and yet betrayed and misunderstood. The *nomos* of love is in fact betrayed by those who misunderstand the crucifixion and degrade the love professed in life by Jesus to the compassionate love for the one who died on the cross: what, if not this, does Nietzsche's peremptory statement 'Christianity died on the cross' mean?[9] The cross was not accepted for what it was intended to be, that is, as the revelation of the authentic meaning of 'sacrifice', and ended up sweeping away the very word of love inherent in Jesus' message, and therefore reduced, through resentment and the will to vengeance, to compassionate love[10] for the victim that we all, in this perspective, would be: a simply reactive love that evidently prevents any tension and will to create. From here, Nietzsche can take that shattered and broken love, vilified and betrayed in compassionate love, and bring it back to earth beyond any metaphysical distinction.

Sacrifice

As said, the theme of 'sacrifice' is linked in the fourth part to the idea of 'hospitality', in an interweaving that unravels only starting from an understanding of the wider dynamics of the gift implemented by Zarathustra.

The religious meaning of the gift that we find in the 'sacrifice' as a still ineffective gift to God, is not entirely absent in hospitality, that particular relationship that obliges me to offer to the other close to me or my dwelling place, and who, in reciprocating or not my offer of hospitality and my hospitable gifts, is revealed as a friend or enemy: a real test, that of hospitality, to which Zarathustra intends to subject the higher men he has attracted to himself through the 'honey sacrifice'.

As already mentioned, the initial term for *hospes* is *hostis* and finds its correspondent in the Gothic *gasts*; now, while the meaning of *gasts* is 'guest', that of *hostis* is 'enemy'. And it is here that we find the link to be clarified and which depends on the meaning and dynamics of the gift of hospitality: to explain the relationship between 'guest' and 'enemy' it is usually acknowledged that both derive from the meaning of 'foreigner', still attested in Latin; from here there is a possible distinction between 'favourable foreigner' who is therefore the 'guest' and 'hostile foreigner' who is, in fact, the one who reveals himself to be an 'enemy'. *Hostis* is first and foremost the 'foreigner' because he is 'recognised as having equal rights to those of Roman citizens'.[11] The foreigner is not, therefore, the foreigner in general, but rather, to be precise, the one who enters into a relationship through the exchange of gifts:[12] it can be understood, therefore, how the foundation of the institution of hospitality resides precisely in the 'relationship of compensation' that is established between host and guest. When the exchange of gifts is not respected, the host becomes hostile, an enemy.

Through the 'honey sacrifice', Zarathustra attracts the higher men in the hope that they will be able to reciprocate the gift that he is giving them. Initially Zarathustra is convinced that they can reciprocate the gift, that is to say they know how to take positive *action* regarding the wisdom of Zarathustra, that they know how to speak to him about the Over-man and give themselves to the necessary decline, but almost immediately he realizes their inability to reciprocate. As potential friends they show their 'hostility' in this inadequacy, they are not able to reciprocate that 'friend to friend' love that Zarathustra thought he could achieve through them. The long *cry for help* that had distressed Zarathustra as he came back down in order to gather to him the higher men through the cunning of the 'honey sacrifice', now comes directly from his cave where they have found shelter.[13]

> But you cannot guess *what* makes my heart so mischievous –
>
> You yourselves are responsible, and how you look, forgive me! After all, everyone who looks at a despairing person becomes mischievous. To give encouragement to someone who despairs – for that everyone thinks they're strong enough.
>
> You yourselves gave me this strength – a good gift, my elevated guests! A righteous gift for your host! Well then, don't be angry now when I offer you something of my own. (*KSA*, IV, 347)[14]

The higher men gathered in the cave in a relationship of hospitality, with their own desperation they somehow *offer* to Zarathustra who draws new inspiration in communicating his wisdom. He has offered security and refreshment to the higher men and now he would like to receive from them a host's gift that can reciprocate his message/gift, he would like to hear from them words that move towards the Over-man:

This host's gift I beg of your love, that you speak of my children. It is for this that I am rich, for this that I became poor:

[. . .] – what would I not give just to have this one thing: *these* children, *this* living plantation, *these* life-trees of my will and my highest hope! (*KSA*, IV, 351)[15]

But the exchange of gifts that one would like to activate here is already compromised by the love relationship that accompanies it. The cry of despair that comes from the cave signals that Zarathustra's love for them is still necessarily a compassionate love, it could not be otherwise: although aware of the 'death of God', they live fully in that opposition between high and low and they cannot find any security outside that schema. Their despair is the extreme temptation for Zarathustra: with their cry for help they ask to be saved in their individuality and in the separateness in which they live and prosper (another character of their superiority is in fact their 'position' acquired within that separateness to which they still tend to return) without knowing how to go beyond. The higher men never present themselves as 'friends' linked by their common ambition to overcome; on the contrary, they are an obstacle to the overcoming and, because of their thirst for security, they are unable to inspire anything but compassion: that compassionate love that Zarathustra feels in himself as a last temptation and that signals their insuperable distance from the 'new love'. Shut in their individuality and isolation, the higher men do not grasp the words of Zarathustra and end up idolizing the donkey that brays, thus twisting the meaning of the *sacred say yes* (the 'supreme action' of the *Dionysian*) and holding it in a still metaphysical distinction – clearly highlighted by the words of the old pope – that prevents love for the all and therefore for the Over-man.

'But what are you doing, you mortal children?' he cried, as he pulled the praying men off the floor and to their feet. 'Watch out that someone other than Zarathustra should see you:

Anyone would conclude that with your new faith you were the most
vicious blasphemers or the most foolish of all old little women!

And you yourself, you old pope, how can you reconcile for yourself that
you worship this ass here as God?'

–'Oh Zarathustra,' responded the pope, 'forgive me, but in matters of God
I am more enlightened even than you. And that's how it should be. Better to
worship God in this form, than in no form at all!' (*KSA*, IV, 390)[16]

The nostalgia that pervades the whole of *Thus Spoke Zarathustra* and especially
these last pages is due to the modality that accompanies Zarathustra's gift: it is
always a gift of love, yet it is constantly looking for the friend who is able to stay
in that relationship and adequately reciprocate. As 'guests' who do not know
how to reciprocate the gift, higher men prove to be 'hostile' to Zarathustra's
role, but his compassionate love for them does not turn into resentment or
hatred;[17] they are nevertheless welcomed in the Love for the All, in that form
of love which is also love for the 'enemy', who is an obstacle and yet stimulates
the overcoming.

This is also effectively confirmed by the presence among Zarathustra's
guests of the 'ugliest human being', the one who killed God, as he too is worthy
of being hosted in Zarathustra's cave. In the context that leads to the arrival of
the Over-man, of the indistinct, even the greatest aberration is admitted. That
total and unreserved love for the Over-man who will come, gives meaning to
what is and what has been.

But that the higher men are incapable of reciprocating the gift testifies at the
same time to the difficulty of access to the Over-man and the proximity of this
event for each of us. The testing of the higher men clarifies the meaning of the
love 'from friend to friend' which must constitute the relationship on which
it is possible to access the Beyond man, that is, to overcome distinctions. The
higher men are not in themselves the friend that Zarathustra indicates, they
are not in themselves capable of that friendship, because they are too pervaded
by their individuality and too afraid of losing it. The half-broken remain as

such outside the love relationship, indeed in that separation, in that fracture, they figuratively perpetuate the distinction between the ideal world and the apparent world and beyond that they do not know how to proceed.

> Nor are you beautiful enough for me and wellborn. I need clean, smooth mirrors for my teachings; on your surfaces even my own image is distorted.
>
> Your shoulders are weighed down by many a burden, many a memory; in your corners many a wicked dwarf crouches. There is hidden rabble in you as well.
>
> And even if you are higher and of a higher kind: much in you is crooked and deformed. There's no smith in the world who could hammer you right and straight for me.
>
> You are mere bridges – may higher people stride across on you! (*KSA*, IV, 350–1)[18]

Higher men are not 'noble' enough to separate themselves from themselves, to empty themselves of their subjectivity and be filled with new wisdom. Of the three metamorphoses that lead Zarathustra on the road to the Over-man – the camel of the 'you must', the lion of the 'I want' and the child of the 'I am' – the image with which the fourth and last book closes is not the child at all, but significantly the lion with which the last temptation, compassion for the higher men, is conquered,[19] and the search for the friend can begin in the name of the new love and the Over-man. The path is not completed at all, the road is simply marked but requires new companions,[20] others await Zarathustra on the mountains ready to continue his donation, '– for higher, stronger, more victorious, more cheerful ones, [. . .] *laughing lions* must come!' (*KSA*, IV, 351).[21] The figure of the lion with which *Zarathustra* ends is the invitation to become 'laughing lions', friends of Zarathustra in the common exhortation to the advent of the child's 'I am': the seal of eternity understood as fullness and perfection in which every distinction is resolved and every 'I want' coincides with a (unique) higher will. The 'I want' of the lion has the task of awakening the conscience hidden in each of us, a co-belonging that binds us to totality and knows no separation and that above all prevents us from remaining in our separateness and solitude. The lion, too, must in fact be overcome so that the lightness and innocence of the child may be achieved. Freed from the burden of the morality of 'you must', aware therefore of the 'death of God', higher men are not yet capable of affirming the will of the lion and intend to drag their existence away from a new 'metaphysical' hypothesis. The companions and friends of Zarathustra reveal themselves as those who are capable of affirming their will and at the same time know how to separate themselves from it,[22] so that from that detachment (which is contempt from the start and then definitive oblivion of oneself) the innocence of the becoming represented by the 'I am' of the child ('*Unschuld ist das Kind und Vergessen*') which announces the Over-man can rise.

Detachment and transformation

With its development and its outcome, the fourth part of *Zarathustra* therefore shows how the way to the Over-man is not a private affair of higher men, but rather a message 'for all and for none', that is to say, it is potentially accessible to everyone and not only to an elite because everyone has the possibility of renouncing themselves and opening up to the depths of their soul in the co-belonging of the All that they have removed, but at the same time it is a message 'for none' simply in the sense that those who accept it fully have to renounce their individuality and therefore themselves. This is why the gift from friend to friend gives back the love relationship on which this dynamics aimed at overcoming can be grafted. The friend is the one who knows how to renounce himself, and when he gives, I have no obligation to him because it is as if I were receiving from the depths of my own soul. In the friend, in whom I see myself again if I enter into a full relationship with him, there is that nobility[23] that makes him able to empty himself and give up his subjectivity.

The same nobility that, moreover, in *Zarathustra* Nietzsche recognizes in Jesus in the very speech that precedes 'On the Bestowing Virtue'.

> Believe me, my brothers! He died too early; he himself would have recanted his teaching if he had reached my age! He was noble enough for recanting!
>
> But he had not yet matured. A youth loves immaturely, and immaturely too he hates mankind and earth. Still tethered and heavy to him are his mind and the wings of his spirit.
>
> But in a man there is more child than in a youth, and less melancholy; he knows more about death and life. (*KSA*, IV, 95)[24]

In the 'nobility' that Zarathustra recognizes in Jesus ('*Edel genug war er zum Widerrufen!*') lies the possibility of separating oneself from oneself, of renouncing one's own individualization in order to give oneself and reunite with the ground (*Grund*) of the earth that is the unfounded grounding (*Abgrund*) of one's soul: a possibility that, however, according to Nietzsche, Jesus did not bring to fruition and was indeed prevented from doing so by the theological misrepresentation of his doctrine of life. This discourse 'On Free Death', as well as anticipating the themes of *The Antichrist* in which Nietzsche reiterates the merits of Jesus's preaching by contrasting them with the theological misunderstanding created by Paul's reading, lays out in fact the meaning of the decline that gives the new dawn, overcoming, however, that sacrificial reading of the death of Jesus that betrayed his doctrine.

> In your dying your spirit and your virtue should still glow, like a sunset around the earth; or else your dying has failed you.
>
> Thus I myself want to die, so that you my friends love the earth more for my sake; and I want to become earth again, so that I may have peace in the one who bore me. (*KSA*, IV, 95)[25]

Going back to the relationship of friendship as a dynamics capable of leading back to the ground of the earth that coincides with the *Grund der Seele* (grounding/bottom of the soul), Nietzsche here makes the transition to the 'bestowing virtue', intending it as a necessary movement[26] to facilitate the arrival and overcoming of the Over-man. It is a further invitation to accept in an appropriate way the gift of wisdom and love that requires a 'detachment' from one's own ego and a subsequent 'transformation' of those who receive and accept it, according to a process not unlike what Meister Eckhart describes in relation, however, to the acceptance of the gift of grace. The way men must prepare themselves to accept Zarathustra's gift is in fact very reminiscent of the characteristics of the *nobleman* described by Eckhart.

Zarathustra's gift is in some way comparable, even with all the necessary precautions, to the free gift par excellence, the gift of grace, with the only great difference being that in that case the donor is identified in a God as Lord of a separated world, while here the *Who* of the gift is completely missing.[27] The gift does not identify Zarathustra as a real donor but a simple mediator of a wisdom that emerges on the surface like a repressed memory of the earth that everyone has in common: that *Chaos des Alls* that, as a general character of being,[28] needs to awaken in itself – overcoming one's individuation – in order to be able to give birth-generate a dancing star.[29]

In this parallel of Zarathustra's gift with the gift of grace, we find some decisive points in common. The gift of grace is a gift for all and for none: for everyone, in the sense that everyone can be the recipient of that gift whose reason lies exclusively in God's will, and for none in the sense that with their own strength no one can attain that gift for themselves without God's intervention. In both cases, however, man can prepare himself to accept the prospective gift. Just as in the gift of grace, he can prepare himself to accept God, thus the higher man can make himself a friend, that is, he can 'break himself' so that the *Übermensch* can be born from him. In both cases one can highlight that 'detachment' from the self (*Abgeschiedenheit, Gelassenheit*) which Meister Eckhart describes for the acceptance of the gift of grace:

He should resign himself to begin with, and then he has abandoned all things. In truth, if a man gave up a kingdom or the whole world and did not give up self, he would have given up nothing.[30]

To understand this step, which is fully accomplished in the abandonment of God himself, it is opportune to read it together with the answer that Jesus gives to the Greeks gathered to see him, to get to know him:

> Unless a kernel of wheat falls to the ground and dies, it remains only a single seed. But if it dies, it produces many seeds. Anyone who loves their life will lose it, while anyone who hates their life in this world will keep it for eternal life. (Jn 12.24-25)

The theme of abandoning one's individuality, one's pride, the bonds (even family ties) that characterize an individual, is very recurrent in Jesus's preaching; it is a continuous exhortation to true life (transformed and full),[31] possible only through 'detachment' from one's subjectivity and from what is connected to it.

In Eckhart's thought, 'detachment' means becoming similar to God, and in fact at the end of the process of 'detachment' one reaches the ground of the soul, recognized as an unfathomable depth, not as a metaphysical foundation but as the 'place' of God's birth in man, that is, as the place of the generation of the *Logos*. As Vannini observes,

> in Eckhart detachment is equivalent to love, understood as the end of every passion [. . .]; it is a joyful and almost ecstatic forgetting oneself, to go out of oneself as a small, accidental, psychological self, to find oneself in a dimension that is no longer one's own [. . .], but that is universal: that dimension where 'its boundaries being only light and love'. (Dante, *Paradise*, XXVIII, 54)[32]

And that is what Our Lord meant by these words, that 'a nobleman went forth', for a man must go out from all forms and from himself, become wholly foreign and remote from them all, if he really means to receive the Son and become the Son in God's bosom and heart.[33]

The emptiness produced by the abandonment of one's individuality is filled at the ground of the soul by the richness of God himself[34] through grace. On the other hand, in Nietzsche such a form of 'detachment' is reached by those who, in front of the *Ab-Grund*, that is, in front of the abyss that opened with the 'death of God', do not identify other metaphysical handholds, but rather abandon themselves to the common belonging to the All, renounce themselves (their own subjectivity as the last metaphysical bulwark) and can thus accept Zarathustra's exorbitant message, and like him become a 'transformed', so that from that necessary transformation the *Übermensch*, the *semper adveniens*, may one day be born.

Therefore *Entbildung-Überbildung*, plundering and transformation.[35] Just as for Eckhart the dual concepts exemplify the promotion-acceptance of God's gift of love, so in the same way it sums up the destiny of those who know how to accept Zarathustra's gift of love.

The event

Just as the *nobleman*, in the *Logos* generated in the depths of the soul, remains open to God and to being, holding nothing for himself and abandoning himself to the love of God, in a similar way the *friend*, who announces the possibility, in each, of the Over-man who will come, announces himself as a new opening of being, a 'place' without space that loves totality, that accepts everything and holds nothing for himself. The Over-man is to be understood, in fact, as an extreme symbol for a new ontological conception that may come after the 'death of God', that is, on the unfounded grounding that through it has revealed itself 'historically'. The will to power transvalued in the will to love and create presents a 'being' that in fact coincides with the 'becoming' and that therefore does not stand beyond the threshold like an (empty) archetype to imitate. The new 'being', emptied of its absolute foundations and free from the logic of the *Grund*, knows how to act its *Entbildung* (plundering) without remaining inert in a desperate nihilism.

Making the void in itself and preparing itself for the filling and the continuous 'donation', it is disposed to accept and recreate the new sense of being, the Over-man: an unrepresentable figure that signifies the becoming of man and his continuous transcendence, but that refers first of all to a more general ontological event.

'Detachment' and 'transformation' are still not enough to define Zarathustra's gift of love and wisdom. The love that the friend is capable of awakening in me, opens me to welcome the gift of wisdom, but it must be continued and acted upon so that it can be truly accepted. 'I love the one whose soul squanders itself, who wants no thanks and gives none back: for he always gives and does not want to preserve himself' (*KSA*, IV, 17)[36] we read in the Prologue in *Zarathustra*, but the passage is completed only in the *sense* that it is assigned to that giving to which the soul opens up. In accepting the eternal recurrence of the same, it does not mean closing the giving within a circle, as the passage from the 'Prologue' just mentioned[37] seems to prefigure, since this would in fact prevent that 'will to create' which is the determining aspect of Zarathustra's love aimed at overcoming the abyss opened by the 'death of God'.

> See what fullness is around us! And from such superabundance it is beautiful to look out upon distant seas.
>
> Once people said God when they gazed upon distant seas; but now I have taught you to say: overman.
>
> God is a conjecture, but I want that your conjecturing not reach further than your creating will.
>
> Could you create a god? – Then be silent about any gods! But you could well create the overman. (*KSA*, IV, 109)[38]

The eternal recurrence is the hypothesis that restores eternity understood as the fullness and perfection of being, and only from this fullness, strengthened by the bond of love that holds in unity the totality dispersed in the multiplicity of individualities, is it possible to proceed to the 'creation' of the *Übermensch*.

Oh how then could I not lust for eternity and for the nuptial ring of rings –
the ring of recurrence!

Never yet have I found the woman from whom I wanted children, unless
it were this woman whom I love: for I love you, oh eternity! *For I love you,*
oh eternity! (KSA, IV, 290)[39]

The tension to the Over-man that Zarathustra brings as a gift, is but the
adherence to love for the all that overcomes all partiality and all property. It
is a love that in no way denies the love professed in life by Jesus, but rather
continues it and extends it to the natural sphere that remained on the margins
of an anthropocentric spiritualization: as Jullien observes on the basis of
Zumstein's commentary on John's Gospel, 'to *spiritualise* in John means to pass
from the being-in-life of beings (their *psyché*) to what actually renders them
alive (as *zoé*)',[40] with a possible and desirable openness to creation and to the
beyond the limits of man. The Over-man is not in fact to be understood as
the result of an anthropological improvement, but rather the extension of the
limits of man – 'undetermined animal' and precisely for this reason capable of
extending its boundaries – to the totality of nature: it is a continuous aspiration
that has in some ways the features of Emerson's *Oversoul* and concerns the
ontological level even before the purely anthropological one. By aspiring to the
Over-man it is not simply a matter of making a better, stronger, more powerful
man. The Over-man is rather a human '*typus*' that exemplifies and summarizes
in the renewed (indeed desired) relationship of man with nature,[41] with the
totality, an overall ontological vision[42] that 'accepts' the being in its becoming
and, recognizing its procedural nature, is willing to accept the event in its
happening and actively respond to it, recreating it.

Just as Christianity frees us from the notion of cause and Jesus in fact
'happens', constituting the possible event that bursts in to revolutionize the
ontological level even before the anthropological level,[43] so the Over-man is
not the outcome of a cause but is the possibility that can take place, that can
indeed happen, the event for which we must *actively* prepare ourselves, that is,

prepare our openness to the becoming, to the happening of being, to its events-based 'nature'. In this lies the always *adveniens* character of the Over-man that prevents it from being read as the outcome and final stage of a dialectical process. With respect to the coming of Christ, the continuous tension to the Over-man, combined with the hypothesis (which always remains so) of the eternal recurrence of the same, has the function of 'redeeming' from the past by inhibiting every unchangeable, every stable foundation, and thus make possible the openness to becoming, that is to say, to the giving of being in its happening, outside of any eschatology and any ontotheological vision.[44] The continuous *recreation* desired by Nietzsche completes and perfects the Gospel message with the reference to the 'natural' which integrates with the 'spiritual' and prevents us from seeing in this partiality the privileged access to the totality. It is nature's way to make the ontotheological approach fail: by always including within itself 'productivity' and 'products' together, that is the concept of *physis* as the source and becoming origin of being and the definition of nature as the 'sum of all things', nature makes the figure of the grounding impossible and prevents us from thinking of a creator separate from creation. In this sense, Nietzsche's 'will to create' is freed from the hypothesis of God and restored to man as an integral and *active* part of nature in its process. Rather than creation, it is now opportune to speak of a continuous 'recreation', a term that refers to the Christian tradition but which finds a complete form beyond the metaphysical hypothesis of God. For Thomas, for example, early creation took place on the part of the Father through the Word (*Summa Theologiae* III, 3) and the revelation is the *recreatio* in Christ who responds to the *creatio* by completing and perfecting it in a clear reference to Paul: 'if anyone is in Christ, the new creation has come: The old has gone, the new is here! All this is from God, who reconciled us to himself through Christ' (2 Cor. 5.17-18). In Christ (and in *Imitatio Christi*) recreation is carried out (Gal. 6.15: 'what counts is the new creation'),[45] but this recreation must be freed from the original ontotheological creation, that is, from the hypothesis of a separate God who has in fact put the world into being for the first time. From this point of view, the 'positive'[46] of *revelatio* does not refer to a separate and distant origin to imitate, but to the very course of becoming in which we have always been placed. Recreation, therefore, without ontotheological creation, without separateness and without metaphysical distinctions, such is Nietzsche's 'will to create' insomuch as it is the will to give meaning to what makes no sense, since it lacks an original cause.

On the other hand, it is precisely through the continuous tension to the *semper adveniens* Over-man combined with the hypothesis of the eternal recurrence, that Nietzsche achieves two results that are closely connected. By exhorting a praxis that accepts that tension and acts upon it, he prevents, first of all, interpreting the Over-man as the result of a spiritual abandonment to the fusion with the all, and, secondly, he makes possible that (albeit partial) self-preservation that is necessary to preserve in the continuous gift, to which he also extends an invitation. The law of love that requires one to give oneself completely is, in fact, 'impossible' precisely because it leads – if fully accepted – to one's depletion, to one's final decline: the 'tension' to the Over-man, which 'directs' the *continuous* giving of oneself, paradoxically allows one to save oneself *in* the decline itself, in the common and solitary path (that *Gang* which, as Zarathustra says, coincides with your/our *Untergang*) which is always possible in its happening (in its *event*) because it has always been rooted in the depths of each person's soul as a possibility of 'detachment' and 'transformation'. A paradoxical 'community of solitary people' is what emerges with Zarathustra's gift, in the definition of a sort of *star friendship* oriented to the birth of the Over-man.[47] Only in these terms is it legitimate to speak of a particular form of evolving *communitas* that goes beyond the nihilistic (passive) *immunitas* without, however, being able in any way to translate itself into some form of (stable) politics, since the State is also a metaphysical form to be overcome in the continuous tension to the *beyond* man.[48] The bond of this *star friendship* lies rather in the common belonging to the all and the possible common 'response' to Zarathustra's gift. In this (common) tension that does not completely break those who are willing to follow it, the openness to the event and to the (re)creation of the Over-man, always *adveniens* but always possible 'here and now', is prepared in clear continuity with the teachings of Jesus, who exhorts a full life, and in polemical response to the theological misunderstanding of his message.

> True life, eternal life has been found—it is not promised, it is there, it is *in you* [es ist da, es ist in *euc*]: as life in love, in love without abatement, and exemption, without distance. (*KSA*, VI, 200)[49]
>
> When the centre of gravity of life is placed, not in life, but in the 'other world' – in nothingness – life has in reality been deprived of its centre of gravity. (*KSA*, VI, 217)[50]

Afterword

The friendship to come

Dort, wo der Staat aufhört, – so seht ümir doch hin, meine Brüder!
Seht ihr ihn nicht, den Regenbogen und die Brüken des Übermenschen?

F. Nietzsche, Also sprach Zarathustra, Von neuen Götzen[1]

One can say that the only adequate response to Zarathustra's gift basically coincides with the friendship between those who feel united in the common tension to the Over-man. This offers the only possibility to continue the dynamics that the 'gift' triggers: that virtue that (eternally) gives and that knows how to lead beyond man and his miseries, beyond the individual and his loneliness, beyond the idea of possession and restitution that corrodes a certain 'terrestrial' friendship, which still lives on distinctions and contrasts and that must be overcome and revolutionized in the direction of that friendship to come that Nietzsche calls 'star friendship'. In this common tension, which is above all of an ethical nature, the Political remains in the background as a simple opportunity for encounter, always revisable and articulated in different ways. The friendship to which Nietzsche aspires has no clear vision of a form of government for a community of friends: it is friendship itself, because of its intimate paradoxicality, that prevents a stable political form, and this applies all the more to the friendship that unites in the direction of the Over-man.

In his book *The Politics of Friendship*, Jacques Derrida dwells at length on the meaning of the apostrophe 'O, my friends, there is no friend', attributed to Aristotle but taken up and developed by many authoritative thinkers, to underline, through the evident paradoxicality of the expression, how the authentic relationship of friendship, rather than representing a stable bond (*bébaios*) – which is the view of the political practice that believes it is constantly used as the basis of and link for every community – lives instead on a precarious balance and is in fact more future-oriented (if possible) than a relationship to be created and regenerated day by day. The expression 'O, my friends, there is no friend' has, as said, an intrinsic paradoxicality: addressed to a group of (supposed) friends, it emphatically denies the existence of the friends themselves. In so doing, the apostrophe hides within itself a hope and an augury for a higher and rarer friendship, but at the same time it recognizes the existence of a (provisional, to be reviewed and improved?) friendly relationship – that is, it recognizes the existence of a host of 'friends' who are potentially capable of listening to the lament and appeal for a higher and more authentic friendship that is still and always to come.

Beyond the descriptions offered by Aristotle about *first friendship* (*pròtè philía*) and the investigation into the legitimacy of attributing the famous phrase to Aristotle, the apostrophe 'O, my friends, there is no friend', to which Derrida constantly refers in his book, emphasizes not only the rarity of an authentic relationship of friendship, but even seems intent on a higher friendship still to be achieved. The rarity and singularity of friendship (aspects on which Aristotle dwells explicitly in his works on ethics) are in fact not capable of summarizing and exhausting the scope of the deepest allusion contained in the expression in question: this translates, in fact, into a sort of lament-call addressed to those who 'so far' can *only improperly* be called friends and are not 'yet' authentically so; this is not simply due to a shortcoming within them, but rather to the paradoxical nature inherent in friendship itself, which, while referring to the always becoming nature of the relationship, requires at the same time that stability and sharing among many people that is not consistent with the dynamics of friendship and its rarity.

In Derrida's aspirations – indeed not as clear in his book as his sharp deconstructive reflections are – friendship should still be firmly linked to a political destiny, all still to be created and then preserved, oriented towards the creation of a new form of democracy governed by equality and freedom. This stance, in fact, echoes Aristotle's traditional approach which inextricably links *philia* and *koinonìa* (friendship and community), already highlighting the difficulties present in this juxtaposition which seeks to keep the singularity and rarity of authentic friendship together with the sharing between many in a community context. For Aristotle, 'friendship consists [in fact] in community' (*Etica Nicomachea*, 1159b, 30–4), since it is based on a close agreement between people who can call themselves friends precisely because they see themselves as united in an association, in a community. Now, if it is true as stated in *Politics* that 'every State is a community' (*Politics*, I, 1252), this does not at all mean that every form of community must necessarily be political (that is a *koinonia politiké*): the community established on the basis of friendship is first of all an association of an ethical character that can certainly be subsequently confirmed in the stability typical of a political union without this passage being taken as being necessary. What characterizes every community of friends is in fact the evidence that it is first of all 'established with a view to some good' (*Politics*, I, 1252): this tension towards an end (*télos*), which animates friendship and the community that rests on it, can certainly take place in a union of a political nature, but it needs a stability and durability over time that friendship in its intrinsic problematic nature and its aspiration to a higher and rarer form based on freedom and equality cannot in itself guarantee. It is within these folds that Derrida can suggest, making partial use of Nietzschean criticism as well, a new form of democratic political association that echoes the notion of friendship in its most problematic sense and which is constantly looking towards a possible future, but all still to come.

If it is true, therefore, that a generic form of 'friendship' can be said to be at the basis of any political unity, then the tension that animates authentic friendship must be considered, in my opinion, first of all on the ethical level, since here we do not see – as is the case with the Political – the necessary contrast to the 'enemy' in order to identify the 'friend', but rather there is an insistence on a common end (or good) that binds and keeps friends together without the need to oppose anything. On the other hand, it is always on this level, the ethical one, that the rethinking of the Political is also played out, starting from a general rethinking of friendship as a privileged form of social relationship.

The difficulty in discussing friendship as the bond at the base of the political community is effectively demonstrated in the work of Carl Schmitt – to whom Derrida makes significant reference – who, in his *The Concept of Political*, points out how in the friend/enemy pair, identified as being at the basis of political unity and conflict, it is always opportune to start from enmity and not friendship to define the Political. He maintains, in fact, that 'there is no Political without the enemy', nor is it possible to automatically define friendship as the simple 'opposite' of enmity. The fact that within the friend/enemy pair, Schmitt, the philosopher of politics, chooses without hesitation to start from the 'enemy' to define the Political and not from the 'friend', testifies to the difficulty of defining friendship, its boundaries and its extension, as the foundation of the political community. This choice reveals, on the one hand, how all the variants and nuances contained in friendship would make the definition of the Political very unclear and, on the other, how the simplified definition of enmity cannot in any case clarify *nor contradict* what is meant by friendship.

That the destiny of friendship is played out within the political or ethical role it holds is also confirmed in Derrida's long and articulated reflections that follow – at least for a significant part – Nietzsche's theses and then separate from them on the very threshold of the definition of a still 'political' meaning of friendship. For Derrida, a general rethinking of friendship and its paradoxicality should be directed towards a new form of democracy based on equality and freedom. Now, clearly, given his explicit aversion to democracy and its prerogatives, Nietzsche could not have supported a democratic conclusion to the new friendship to come. However, this is not enough to distance Derrida from Nietzsche's thesis about friendship; the distance between the two is even more radical: the tension that animates Nietzsche's reflection on friendship cannot be summed up in any political form. For Nietzsche, rethinking friendship also means rethinking the political dimension in its complexity, so that the tension to the friendship to come cannot be translated into a stable form of government, but rather in a continuous shared tension that can, if anything, find opportunities for solidifying without the dynamics then being interrupted or saturated forever. Nietzsche's position on friendship is basically summed up in this enlightening intuition where the German philosopher understands that in order to access a higher form of friendship it is necessary to overcome the opposition constituted by the idea of the 'enemy':

> And [. . .] *perhaps* each man will some day know the more joyful hour in which he says:
>
>   'Friends, there are no friends!' the dying wise man shouted.
>
>   'Enemies, there is no enemy!' shout I, the living fool.[2]

Read also in the light of Schmitt's reflections on the Political, this passage, which concludes part six of the first book in *Human, All Too Human* with the title 'Man in Society' urges us to think how the 'perhaps' of that happiest hour, in which that hoped-for friendship to come might occur, can take on a concrete form only in the moment the overcoming of enmity is also concomitantly achieved. An overcoming that alludes, on the one hand, to the continuation of Christian love, which must be extended to the enemy, and, on the other hand, to the de-politicization (*Ent-politisierung*) of stable forms of government (we could say in Nietzsche-speak, at the 'death of the State'), which corresponds, however, to the over-politicization typical of a marked individualism in which the individual, who struggles to find communities to identify with or to oppose, takes upon himself in his solitude the reasons for an extreme opposition to the other. In this ragged context, the friendship to come presents itself as the new meaning to be assigned to the earth: a new meaning, which is exactly that tension to the Over-man, which rests, though, on a common and original belonging, repressed and forgotten, however, in the separateness of the individual's solitude and in conflicting simplified relationships that are political (and no longer ethical in the broad sense), in that they conform to the friend/enemy schema: a schema, we have said, that does not in any way allow for a full definition of friendship to be reached. It is in this sense that the desire for the 'living madman' to overcome the 'enemy' that balances and integrates the hope of the 'dying wise man' and urges the extreme overcoming of the bastion of solitude in which the radical and residual enmity that must be eradicated is nested, must be seen. Precisely in Nietzsche's desire for the friendship to come, the need to overcome the two temptations that prevent the realization of Zarathustra's gift of solitude and compassionate love is revived.

In a passage of Nietzsche's echoed by Derrida, how the wise man can pretend to be insane (*Human, All Too Human*, II, 246) when he wants to suggest a direction that is still unexplored yet worthy of being taken and studied, is brought to mind. On that madness, which – as we have said – in the case of the tension to the friendship to come echoes the madness of Christian love that exhorts love for the enemy, Nietzsche 'founds' the new lineage of the philosophers of the future,[3] who, like the madman that announces the 'death of God', say they are (and know they are) friends of the 'truth' that is coming: a 'truth' that obviously escapes all dogmatism and translates, in fact, into a simple aspiration, that is, into a creative tension that is released on the relational plane precisely in the creation of a higher friendship. Nietzsche holds that to think of friendship means, in fact, to accept the instability of the 'perhaps' on which the highest friendship hangs, and to grasp in that instability the continuous tension to the Over-man, who is not a (super)human type to pursue and achieve, but rather is to be understood as an open and dynamic form of relationship between individuals and between individuals and the nature to which they belong.

Genuine friendship as a political *koinonìa* is in itself impossible because, when it is such, it is rare and with difficulty holds a significant number of people actually together (instead there is camaraderie, there can be friendship). Moreover, friendship denies itself because, if it is perfect, it demands that the friend be perfect, not lacking in anything, and that he be, after all, like a God; but a God does not need friends and a God cannot, by definition, live that closeness-proximity which is fundamental to the friendship on which a political community rests.

One point on which the friendship of the *koinonìa* is based is, in fact, its effectiveness, which is expressed in the concrete closeness between friends: a closeness that binds together members of the same community and separates them (through distance) from their enemies. However, in the moment that the friendship to come goes beyond this 'political', 'terrestrial' opposition, even the need for effective proximity disappears. This is what happens in the 'star friendship' evoked by Nietzsche.

> *Star friendship.* We were friends and have become estranged. But this was right, and we do not want to conceal and obscure it from ourselves as if we had reason to feel ashamed. We are two ships each of which has its goal and course; our paths may cross and we may celebrate a feast together, as we did – and then the good ships rested so quietly in one harbor and one sunshine that it may have looked as if they had reached their goal and as if they had one goal. But then the almighty force of our tasks drove us apart again into different seas and sunny zones, and perhaps we shall never see each other again; perhaps we shall meet again but fail to recognize each other: our exposure to different seas and suns has changed us. That we have to become estranged is the law above us; by the same token we should also become more venerable for each other – and the memory of our former friendship more sacred. There is probably a tremendous but invisible stellar orbit in which our very different ways and goals may be *included* as small parts of this path; let us rise up to this thought. But our life is too short and our

power of vision too small for us to be more than friends in the sense of this
sublime possibility. – Let us then *believe* in our star friendship even if we
should be compelled to be earth enemies. (*KSA*, III, 523–4)[4]

What brings Nietzsche's friendship to a meta-political level is the overcoming
of the 'human, all too human' dimension of this relationship, which on the one
hand declines towards the solitude of the individual and on the other would
like to turn towards a compassionate love[5] that, however, blocks the dynamics
of friendship and blocks the virtue that it continually gives and which should
characterize it. As mentioned in the course of the book, by continuing and
overcoming Christian love, Nietzsche intends to integrate it with the love of
the nature and for the nature to which we belong. The enmity with which
Schmitt's Political is given clearly concerns the plane of 'terrestrial' relations
between men,[6] while the 'star' friendship to which Nietzsche refers instead
concerns a higher plane, that is, the recovery of a cosmic unity necessarily
shattered and to be reinvented with the common tension to the Over-man
('We were friends and have become estranged. But this was right, and we do
not want to conceal and obscure it from ourselves as if we had reason to feel
ashamed'). Star friendship is a simple possibility to which we can adhere in
order to overcome – at least temporally – the separateness in which we live:
by accepting the common tension to the Over-man, as a 'good' to which new
friends aspire, we can, according to Nietzsche, orient ourselves towards that
friendship which binds us in distance, so as to make possible a 'community
of solitary people' who conform to a continuous love for the friend which
translates into the continuous dynamics of the bestowing virtue, and which
cannot be hypostatized in a stable political form without losing its continuous
aspiration. This friendship has nothing to do with some kind of political form;
it is about relationships that individuals know and can (re)activate by crossing
the boundaries that separate different communities, different interests, and
different conflicts.

Notes

Introduction

1 H. Melville, *Moby Dick or The Whale* (New York: Penguin Classics, 2002), p. 32.
2 Although of course there are some important exceptions such as H. Alderman, *Nietzsche's Gift* (Athens: Ohio University Press, 1977) and G. Shapiro, *Alcyone: Nietzsche on Gift, Noise and Women* (New York: SUNY, 1991).
3 See H. Arendt, *Love and Saint Augustine (1929)* (Chicago: University of Chicago Press, 1998); R. Bodei, *Ordo amoris. Conflitti terreni e felicità celeste* (Bologna: il Mulino, 1991).
4 See G. Abel, *Nietzsche. Die Dynamik der Willen zur Macht* (Berlin-New York: Walter de Gruyter, 1998); in particular pp. 28–48.
5 In addition to the classics G. Naumann, *Zarathustra Commentar* (Leipzig: Verlag von Haessel, 1899–1901) and H. Weichelt, *Friedrich Nietzsche: Also sprach Zarathustra, Erklärt und gewürdig* (Leipzig: Duerr, 1910) (second edition revised as *Zarathustra-Kommentar* (Leipzig: Meiner, 1922)), see also the excellent commentary by G. Pasqualotto, published together with the Italian edition translated by Sossio Giametta and published by Rizzoli (Milan) in 1988, as well as the important volume dedicated to the interpretation of *Zarathustra* edited by Volker Gerhardt in 2012 for Akademie Verlag and published in the Klassiker Auslegen series. See also S. Giametta, *Commento allo 'Zarathustra'* (Milan: Bruno Mondadori, 1996).

Chapter 1

1 M. Mauss, *The Gift. The Form and Reason for Exchange in Archaic Societies*, trans. by W. D. Halls (London: Routledge, 1990).
2 See É. Benveniste, *Le Vocabulaire des institutions indo-européennes*, 2 vols. (Paris: Minuit, 1969).
3 Ibid., 59 ff.
4 See Mauss, *The Gift*, 14 ff.
5 See C. Lévi-Strauss, 'Introduction à l'œuvre de Mauss' in M. Mauss, *Sociologie et Anthropologie* (Paris: PUF, 1950).

6 See J. T. Godbout, *L'espri du don* (Montréal-Paris: Éditions La Découverte, 1992), 157 ff; see also M. Aime, 'Da Mauss al MAUSS', the introduction to the Italian ed. of M. Mauss, *Saggio sul dono (The Gift)* (Turin: Einaudi, 2002), XIV–XVI.

7 On the rich subject of recognition, I refer in particular to Axel Honneth's excellent studies: *Kampf um Anerkennung – Zur moralischen Grammatik sozialer Konflikte* (Frankfurt am Main: Suhrkamp, 1994), *Das Ich im Wir: Studien in Anerkennungstheorie* (Frankfurt am Main: Suhrkamp, 2010) and *Anerkennung. Eine europäische Ideengeschichte* (Frankfurt am Main: Suhrkamp, 2018).

8 See A. Fabris, *Relazione: una filosofia performativa* (Brescia: Morcelliana, 2016); see also ibid., *TeorEtica. Filosofia della relazione* (Brescia: Morcelliana, 2010).

9 See R. Bodei, *La vita delle cose* (Rome-Bari: Laterza, 2014).

10 The aporia that opens up here and essentially remains open in Christianity between freedom of choice to reciprocate God's gift and grace is one of the critical aspects of Christian love that Nietzsche seeks to overcome from his earliest philosophical attempts.

11 As Massimo Cacciari pointed out, and as we will see later, love for the neighbour includes within it also and above all love of the enemy, which really makes this love 'impossible' and detached from the classical dynamics of donation: 'God loves the *plesios* up to the figure of the enemy. God loves *his* enemy. We are called to love *our* enemies in His image. Any compensatory-rewarding schema is omitted. Nothing requires such love, in its turning towards everyone, but to everyone in the inalienable concreteness of its appearance, of its own face, which in any case is opposed to those it meets', M. Cacciari, '*Drammatica della prossimità*' in E. Bianchi and M. Cacciari, *Ama il prossimo tuo* (Bologna: il Mulino, 2011), 95.

12 This includes the passage from *Imitatio Christi* to *imitatio naturae* already highlighted by Karl Löwith and which I have taken up in my *Volontà d'amore. L'estremo comando della volontà di potenza* (Turin: Rosenberg & Sellier, 2011).

13 See Lucio Anneo Seneca, *De Beneficiis* (62 AD).

14 É. Benveniste, *Le Vocabulaire des institutions indo-européennes*, 49. See also M. Mauss, 'Gift-Gift', in M. Mauss, *Œuvres* (Paris: Minuit), vol. III, pp. 29–103 and J. Starobinski, 'Don fastueux et don pervers', in *Annales E.S.C.*, 41 (1986): 7–26.

15 I developed the theme in my 'Ordo amoris, ordo voluntatis', in *Cristalli di Storicità. Saggi in onore di Remo Bodei*, eds by E. C. Corriero and F. Vercellone (Turin: Rosenberg & Sellier, 2019), 62–75.

16 A. Caillé, *Antropologie du don: Le tiers paradigme* (Paris: Desclée de Brouwer, 2000), 23 ff.

17 Ibid., 8.

18 Ibid., 10.

19 Ibid., 12–13.

20 Speaking of the third paradigm, Caillé and his colleagues at MAUSS in no way claim to reveal an unprecedented discovery, 'on the contrary, everything we enunciate is of great simplicity and has already been formulated, in one form or another, countless times. Many schools, philosophical or sociological, revolve and have revolved around the same issues for a long time' (ibid., 15).

21 See J. T. Godbout, *L'espri du don*, 220 ff.

22 Ibid., 30; Caillé takes Godbout's same narrow definition as the basis for the explanation of the dynamics of the third paradigm, see A. Caillé, *Antropologie du don*, 79 ff.

23 See J. T. Godbout, *L'espri du don*, 217–20 for the 'value of the bond' and 220–33 for the gratuitousness of the gift.

24 É. Benveniste, *Le Vocabulaire des institutions indo-européennes*, 153.

25 Ibid.

26 See D. Vidal, 'Les trois Grâces ou l'allégorie du Don', *Gradhiva*, 9 (1991): 13–47.

27 For Derrida the gift is not *is*, but *is here*, it gives: 'The gift, like the event, as event, must remain unpredictable, but remain so without holding back. It must let itself be structured by risk. [. . .] The gift and the event obey nothing but principles of disorder, that is, principles without principle', J. Derrida, *Donner le temps. La fausse monnaie* (Paris: Galilée, 1991), 122–3; on the subject of the gift, see also J. Derrida, *Donner la mort* (Paris: Galilée, 1999).

28 Ibid., 128.

29 See J.-L. Marion, *Réduction et donation. Recherches sur Husserl, Heidegger et la phénoménologie* (Paris: PUF, 1989).

30 See in particular J.-L. Marion, *Etant donné. Essai d'une phénoménologie de la donation* (Paris: PUF, 1997); see also ibid., *Dialogo con l'amore*, ed. by U. Perone (Turin: Rosenberg & Sellier, 2007). For a general overview of the 'gift' in philosophy, see A. Tagliapietra, *Il dono del filosofo. Sul gesto originario della filosofia* (Turin: Einaudi, 2009).

31 R. Esposito, *Communitas. Origine e destino della comunità* (Turin: Einaudi, 2006), new edition, p. xiii.

32 'Where the state *ends*, look, look, brothers! Can't you see it, the rainbow, and the bridges of the overman?' (*KSA*, IV, 64), F. Nietzsche, 'The New Idol', *Thus Spoke Zarathustra*, ed. by Robert Pippin, trans. by Adrian Del Caro (Cambridge: Cambridge University Press, 2006).

33 Esposito, *Communitas*, 145–62; in particular p. 148.

34 In this regard, Remo Bodei's analyses in his work of the forms of identity are important for understanding the model proposed by Esposito, see R. Esposito, *Lo stemma e il Blasone*, in *Cristalli di Storicità. Saggi in onore di Remo Bodei*, ed. by E. C. Corriero and F. Vercellone (Turin: Rosenberg & Sellier), 2019, 30 ff.

35 See Benveniste, *Le Vocabulaire des institutions indo-européennes*, 64–75.

36 'Hospitality is clarified by the reference to the *potlatch* of which it is an attenuated form. It is based on the idea that one man is bound to another (*hostis* always has a reciprocal value) by the obligation to compensate for a certain service he has received', Benveniste, *Le Vocabulaire des institutions indo-européennes*, 69.

Chapter 2

1 'The figs fall from the trees, they are good and sweet; and as they fall, their red skin ruptures. I am a north wind to ripe figs', F. Nietzsche, 'On the Blessed Isles', *Thus Spoke Zarathustra*.

2 ' – Among my writings my Zarathustra stands alone. With it I have given humanity the greatest gift it has ever been given. [. . .] Here speaks no "prophet", none of those gruesome hybrids of sickness and will to power called founders of religions. Above all you have to hear properly the tone that comes out of this mouth, this halcyon tone, if you are not to be pitifully unjust towards the meaning of its wisdom. "It is the stillest words that bring on the storm; thoughts that come on doves' feet direct the world—"' F. Nietzsche, *Sämtliche Werke. Kritische Studienausgabe*, ed. by G. Colli and M. Montinari (Berlin-New York: Walter de Gruyter, 1967–1977 and 1988) (*KSA*, vol. VI, p. 269); F. Nietzsche, 'Foreword', *Ecce Homo*. For the Italian translation of Nietzsche's works I refer to the edition *Opere*, ed. by G. Colli and M. Montinari (Milan: Adelphi, 1964 ff), referring where possible simply to the work and the paragraph. On the use of the adjective 'halcyon' in relation to the gift, see G. Shapiro, *Alcyone: Nietzsche on Gift, Noise, and Women* (Albany: SUNY, 1991), 1–51: 'Let us recall that Alcyone who gives her name to "the halcyon", was transformed into a sea bird when she desperately willed to follow Ceyx, her drowned husband [during a storm caused by the gods to punish their happiness]. And as a result of this transformation, the sea observes an annual period of calm each year so that the halcyon (kingfisher) birds can hatch their eggs in those miraculous floating nests', ibid., 16. Dedicated to Thetis, the halcyon represents a connection between heaven and earth, and it is easy to find, in the silence that enables their reproduction, those 'stillest words' that carry with them the 'storm' (that storm for which Ceyx and Alcyone died and were 'transformed') that can generate new 'transformees'.

3 'To have understood six sentences of that book, that is to have lived them, raises mortals to a higher degree than what "modern" men could achieve' (*KSA* VI, p. 299) writes Nietzsche in reply to Heinrich von Stein who complained that he did not understand a single word of *Zarathustra*. See F. Nietzsche, 'Why I Write Such Excellent Books', *Ecce Homo*.

4 In the letter dated 13 February 1883 that Nietzsche sent from Genoa to his publisher Ernst Schmeitzner, Nietzsche speaks of his now completed book as a 'decisive step': 'it is a "poem" or a "fifth Gospel", or rather something for which there is no name yet' (F. Nietzsche, *Sämtliche Briefe, Kritische Studienausgabe*, vol. VI, 327 ff).

5 In a letter sent in April 1883 to Malwida von Meysenbug, Nietzsche states in fact that he 'challenged all religions' and that he had achieved 'a new "holy book"' with *Zarathustra* (Nietzsche, *Sämtliche Briefe*, vol. VI, 363).

6 The alternation of high and low, deep and shallow, is constant in *Zarathustra* and in itself provides an interesting key to understanding the notion of passage, *Über-gang*, and the notion of decline, *Unter-gang*.

7 R. W. Emerson, *The Collected Works of Ralph Waldo Emerson: The Conduct of Life* (Prague: e-artnow, 2018), n.p.

8 F. Nietzsche, 'Prologue', *Thus Spoke Zarathustra*.

9 F. Nietzsche, *Beyond Good and Evil*, trans. by Helen Zimmern, in *The Complete Works of Friedrich Nietzsche* (Edinburgh-London: T. N. Foulis, 1909).

10 'My concept "Dionysian" here has become the supreme deed [*die höchste That*]' (KSA, VI, 343) (*Ecce Homo*, VI), writes Nietzsche in *Ecce Homo*, his intellectual testament, clarifying how the absence of Dionysus is in fact the testimony of his complete deployment in action – in a decisive step – which Zarathustra exhorts; see F. Nietzsche, *Ecce Homo* and *Thus Spoke Zarathustra*.

11 Dionysus himself, in his triadic development and even more in his form of Iacchus, is a god who somehow prepares and anticipates the coming of Christ. In concrete terms, then, in the effort to overcome Christianity, Nietzsche expressly uses the figure of Dionysus as opposed to the Crucified, that is to say Jesus neutralized in sacrifice, as a common lost line that is to be recovered; for a more in-depth look at the points of contact between Dionysus and Christ, see G. Fornari, *Da Dioniso a Cristo: conoscenza e sacrificio nel mondo greco e nella civiltà occidentale* (Turin: Marietti 1820, 2006), which, even though it is strongly based on the Girardian structure, is an important resource for these themes; I have dealt with them in more depth in the chapter 'Deus sempre adveniens' in my book *Vertigini della ragione. Schelling e Nietzsche* (Turin: Rosenberg & Sellier, 2018), new edition, 155–93.

12 See also Jn 12.27: 'Now my soul is troubled, and what shall I say? "Father, save me from this hour"? No, it was for this very reason I came to this hour. Father, glorify your name!'

13 It is the danger that, for example, the hermit, without knowing how to avoid it, has run into the recluse with whom he is confronted as soon as he descends the mountain.

14 For example, in John's Gospel: 'I and the Father are one' (Jn 10.30); 'Yet I am not
    alone, for my Father is with me' (Jn 16.32).

15 On the subject, I refer to G. Pasqualotto's valuable considerations, *Commento* a
    F. Nietzsche, *Così parlò Zarathustra*, trans. by S. Giametta (Milan: Rizzoli, 1985),
    369–546; here in particular pp. 384–5.

16 'I have not been asked, as I should have been asked, what the name of Zarathustra
    means to me, in my capacity as the first immoralist; for what distinguishes this
    Persian from all the others in the past is the very fact that he was the exact opposite
    of an immoralist' (KSA, VI, 367), F. Nietzsche, 'How One Becomes What One Is',
    Ecce Homo.

17 In an apparent contradiction aimed, instead, at preventing, on the one hand, a
    teleological reading of the tension to the Over-man and, on the other, the banal
    circular vision of time as the solution to the enigma of eternal recurrence. The
    eternity to which the eternal recurrence refers is rather the immanent perfection
    that the unrepresentable image of the Over-man promises in a continuous
    tension that is to be read rather in continuity with Anaximander's saying in
    which each fragment finds a solution in the original totality from which it
    comes and to which it is destined to return. Here, however, Nietzsche sees the
    double risk of a separation between the real world and the apparent world and
    a moral and moralizing view of the world: the proposed solution to overcome
    the separation is to become Heraclitean. Yet, as I have tried to show elsewhere,
    Anaximander's doctrine, if correctly understood, is an *ante litteram* synthesis of
    Parmenides' Being and Heraclitus' becoming: 'If it is true that the ontological
    doctrine described by the *will to power* is ultimately the synthesis of the ontology
    of Parmenides' Being and the ontology of becoming proposed by Heraclitus,
    then it is even more true that they find an *ante litteram* synthesis already in
    Anaximander's saying, if, however, ἄπειρον (*ápeiron*) is intended as the a-topic
    place where one finds the *absolute becoming* without order, rule and form, of
    the Being insofar as it exists, which in turn guarantees the "phenomenological"
    becoming of the entities in so far as they are born, reside and decline; in other
    words, on the basis of a distinction which we have already mentioned between (1)
    the *absolute becoming* of the ἄπειρον and therefore of "what it really is" and (2)
    the "phenomenological" becoming, so to speak, of the entities that "appear" and
    that we perceive through the "sensation", which always and in any case leads to
    the unity of the original Will', E. C. Corriero, *Volontà d'amore*, 74; see in general
    pp. 72–4.

18 F. Nietzsche, 'Prologue', *Thus Spoke Zarathustra*.

19 F. Nietzsche, *The Gay Science*, trans. by Walter Kaufmann (New York: Knopf
    Doubleday Publishing Group – Vintage Books, Kindle Edition, 1974), § 343.

20 *Supra*, FN 12, 117–18.

21 In the sense proposed by Plotinus: 'eternity, that is to say that kind of life without shocks, all together, by now without limits and disbandments, due to the fact that it is placed permanently in the One', *Enneadi* III, 7, 11.

22 As Enzo Bianchi observes, 'the essence of Christianity [is] in the proclamation not only of love that conquers death, but of a free love, called "grace" [. . .]; gratis, free, unconditional, faithful love for eternity. This is the good news, the Gospel: God's love is not to be deserved, it precedes us, it reaches us before we can do anything to deserve it! [. . .] God's love for humanity' (see Jn 3.16: 'For God so loved the world that he gave his one and only Son') is a love that cannot be repaid. As recited by an ancient anaphora that in a single verse gives all the activity originating from gratuitousness: 'We give you thanks, Lord, we your sinful servants to whom you have granted your grace that cannot be repaid (*Anaphora of Addai and Mari*)', in E. Bianchi, *Dono e Perdono* (Turin: Einaudi, 2014), 16–17.

23 'Free will', writes Nietzsche in *Fate and History*, 'appears as unfettered, deliberate; it is boundlessly free, wandering, the spirit. Fate is the boundless force of opposition against free will. Free will without fate is just as unthinkable as spirit without reality, good without evil. Only antithesis creates the quality. [. . .] [F]ree will is nothing but the highest potency of fate', F. Nietzsche, *Fate and History*.

24 F. Nietzsche, 'Prologue', *Thus Spoke Zarathustra*.

25 See in general *Sermon on the Mount* in Mt. 5.1-48, but also the so-called 'sermon on the plain' by Luke (in particular Lk. 6.20-45).

26 The reflections of later philosophical anthropology, in particular Scheler's and Gehlen's, owe much to Nietzsche and are in turn enlightening for this passage of his thought.

27 F. Nietzsche, *Scritti giovanili, 1856-1864*, trans. and ed. by M. Carpitella (Milan: Adelphi, 1998), 213.

28 F. Nietzsche, *Twilight of the Idols and The Anti-Christ*, trans. by Thomas Common (Kansas: Digireads.com Publishing, Kindle Edition, 2018), § 29.

29 Massimo Cacciari highlighted it very well in his essay 'Il Gesù di Nietzsche' in *Micromega*, 1, 2000; see also M. Cacciari, *L'arcipelago* (Milan: Adelphi, 1997), 143–54; on the figure of Jesus in Nietzsche's philosophy see, of course, K. Jaspers, *Nietzsche and Christianity* (Washington: Regnery Company, 1961).

30 Moreover, in continuity with the Gospel passage Mt. 10.8: 'Freely you have received; freely give.'

31 Nietzsche, 'Prologue'.

32 For an overall reading of the passage, I refer to my *Vertigini della ragione*, 99–103.

33 The gift of wisdom is poisonous because in one way it is destined to die, to the decline of individuality, but it is also poisonous in the sense that it is poisoned since it carries with it the risk of a declining and passive doctrine betrayed in its foundation.

Chapter 3

1 E. Dickinson, *Bolts of Melody. New Poems of Emily Dickinson*, eds by Mabel Loomis Todd and Millicent Todd Bingham (New York: Harper, 1945), 1.207.

2 F. Nietzsche, 'The Child with the Mirror', *Thus Spoke Zarathustra*.

3 Ibid.; love for the friend, which is completed only with love for the enemy, is to be read in direct continuity with the authentic love of the neighbour as preached by the Gospels. When Nietzsche proposes the overcoming of the love of the neighbour, he has in mind a figure who is misunderstood and betrayed by the compassionate love that pollutes the love for himself and for the future ('your love of the neighbor is your bad love of yourselves'), but on closer inspection the figure of the friend he proposes in its place has much in common with the *plesios*. See Cacciari, *Drammatica della prossimità*.

4 F. Nietzsche, 'The Child with the Mirror', *Thus Spoke Zarathustra*.

5 That the transvaluation of all values is a kind of *conversio* is explicitly inferred when Nietzsche describes his work as 'a challenge to all religions', thus claiming that he can give meaning to a world that has been discovered to be without meaning.

6 *Supra*, 5–25.

7 On the passage from the will to power to the 'will to love', see my books *Volontà d'amore* (Will to love) and *Vertigini della ragione* (The vertigo of reason): 'Love for the *Übermensch* is a love that goes beyond egoism and dispenses gifts. It is not a compassionate love that 'nails' the beloved in its stability, it is rather a love that still wants to create the beloved object. For Nietzsche, love means giving meaning, and giving meaning is the ultimate form of the will to create. One of Nietzsche's concerns is to save the phenomenological evidence of becoming, and the attempt to emancipate the will to power towards the *will to create* is directed at achieving this. The will to power that has arrived at the "death of God" (that God who served his purpose for so many centuries), is transfigured into the *will to create*, which cannot bear the idea that there is some entity presiding over creation, since it would prevent the absolute Freedom necessary for the creative capacity. The *will to create*, if it is understood in an absolute sense, must be able to address not only the future, but also the present and the past. My *saying yes* must also be able to address what has happened, what is in the past, and to do this Nietzsche proposes the doctrine of the eternal recurrence, which gives meaning to the dispersed totality that is behind us, just as the doctrine of the *Übermensch*, giving meaning to our present, directs us to a future that redeems everything in the past. The future, the kingdom of the *Übermensch*, will in fact justify the All, giving meaning to the fragmented totality, because "by virtue of the supreme idea even the most ignoble objection finds a solution". Each part will recompose itself, not a single element of the Past will be able to object to the All, since each of its moments will have had meaning in the creation of the Over-man: "Let your will say: The Superman *shall be* the meaning of

the earth!'" (KSA, IV, p. 14; F. Nietzsche, 'Prologue', *Thus Spoke Zarathustra*, 3). The *will to create* is, for Nietzsche, the *will to love*: that Love that gives without asking anything in return and that in some ways recalls the Christian *agape*. Corriero, *Vertigini della ragione* (The vertigo of reason), 102–3.

Love is in fact the 'last' word of the will to power, but because of its recursive and affirmative character, love does not describe the 'law' that governs the *Wille zur Macht*, and thus 'defining' it, but simply the option capable of perpetuating its dynamics in the continuous tension to overcoming represented by the Over-man. See also my 'Ordo amoris, ordo voluntatis' in *Cristalli di Storicità. Saggi in onore di Remo Bodei* (Turin: Rosenberg & Sellier, 2019)

8 There most do not believe in God, and the fact that God is dead cannot reach the ears of the unbelievers. They remain tied to the same concept that affirms the existence of God: by denying his existence, they are in the dialectic opposition between being and not-being, without coming up against any kind of contradiction. The madness that knows the 'death of God' needs solitude: 'Flee, my friend, into your solitude! [. . .] Where solitude ends, there begins the marketplace; and where the marketplace begins, there begins too the noise of the great actors, and the buzzing of poisonous flies' (F. Nietzsche, 'On the Flies of the Market Place', *Thus Spoke Zarathustra*). The market is the place where man is the people, and the people need comedians and clowns. Here, to 'upset' means to show, to 'drive crazy' means to convince: a truth that insinuates itself into sharp ears, which here is called falsehood and nothingness. E. C. Corriero, *Il Nietzsche italiano. La 'morte di Dio' e la filosofia italiana del secondo Novecento* (Turin: Aragno, 2016), 106.

9 A diagnosis that is confirmed by Carl Schmitt's speech on the term value with the usual depth of analysis: 'Today, for the common conscience, the term "value" is so impregnated with economic and commercial meaning that there is no turning back. [. . .] The economy, the market and the stock exchange have thus become the terrain for everything that is defined as value in a specific sense. [. . .] The logic of the economic concept of value therefore falls within a rational field of commutative justice, *justitia commutativa*' C. Schmitt, *Die Tyrannei der Werte* (1960); see C. Schmitt, *The Tirrany of Values and Other Texts*, ed. by Russell A. Berman and Samuel Garrett Zeitlin (Candor, NY: Telos Press, 2018). Nietzsche's proposal should not, however, be understood simply as a 'philosophy of life' that determines value from the intensity and accumulation of potential in the subject, nor in a philosophy of *dépense* that attributes value to giving oneself without limit and without reason. Rather, Nietzsche believes that the transvaluation of all values is achieved through the unmasking of the genealogical roots of 'value', and the new 'values' are, if anything, based on the desire to 'give meaning' in/to a world that is known to be meaningless. This will to (give) sense, which is the will to create, finds its aim in love which is in fact to be understood as the extreme *command* (*Befehl*) (or commandment?) of the will to power and turns in the direction of the Over-man.

10 On the enigma of the gift, see S. Rossi, *Oro* (Bologna: il Mulino, 2018), 166 ff; see also A. Quadrio Curzio (ed.), *Oro: storia, protagonisti, problemi* (Roma: Newton Compton, 1989).

11 F. Nietzsche, *Philosophy and Truth: Selections from Nietzsche's Notebooks of the early 1870's*, 1, ed. and trans. by Daniel Breazeale (New Jersey: Humanities Press, 1990).

12 If incomplete nihilism is the simple reversal of values, then 'complete nihilism, on the other hand, must eliminate even the very place of values – the supersensible as a domain – and, in accordance with this, must establish values in a different way and transvalue them. It follows clearly that complete, accomplished and therefore classical nihilism implies, yes, "the transvalorisation of all previous values", but transvalorization is not a mere replacement of old values with new ones. The transvalorizing becomes the crushing and overturning of the type and mode of valorization. The institution of values needs a new principle, that is a new place from which to start and in which to maintain itself. The principle can no longer be the world of the over-sensitive that has become lifeless. The nihilism aimed at transvaluation thus understood, therefore, will be in search of what is most alive. In this way, nihilism itself becomes "the ideal of the afterlife"' (*Will to Power*, aph. 14), M. Heidegger, *Holzwege*, Italian edition ed. by V. Cicero (Milan: Bompiani, 2014), 266; on this subject see F. Vercellone, *Il nichilismo* (Rome-Bari: Laterza, 1996); F. Volpi, *Nichilismo* (Rome-Bari: Laterza, 2009).

13 Recently François Jullien proposed the notion of 'resource' to replace that of 'value', suggesting that what can still be appreciated in Christianity should be read in the light of the 'resources' it can provide more than the 'values' it can sustain and their validity in contemporary society. Jullien's proposal, however, does not seem to be exempt from the reference to a higher value, the subject, which, in fact, identifies resources useful to its qualitative and quantitative extension. Rather, Nietzsche's transvaluation aims to highlight the genealogy of values, their necessity, as well as the possibility of a new position of values based on full nihilistic awareness of the absence of ultimate values. See F. Jullien, *Ressources du christianisme. Mais sans y entrer par la foi* (Paris: L'Herne, 2018), 23–37

14 F. Nietzsche, 'How One Becomes What One Is: Why I am a destiny', *Ecce homo*.

15 Zarathustra's name appeared for the first time among Nietzsche's papers in an aphorism dated 26 August 1881 in connection with the outline for a book that was to have the title *Mittag und Ewigkeit*. Nietzsche is believed to have chosen Zarathustra as his messenger on the back of a passage from Emerson's *Essays* which is underlined in his copy. We read '*Das ist es!* [it's him]' next to the following entry in the volume: 'We require that a man should be so large and columnar in the landscape, that it should deserve to be recorded that he arose, and girded up his loins, and departed to such a place. The most credible pictures are those of majestic men who prevailed at their entrance, and convinced the senses; as happened to the

eastern magian who was sent to test the merits of Zertusht or Zoroaster. "When the Yunani arrived at Balkh," the Persians tell us, "Gushtasp appointed a day on which the Mobeds of every country should assemble, and a golden chair was placed for the Yunani sage. Then the beloved of Yezdam, the prophet Zertusht, advanced into the midst of the assembly. The Yunani sage, on seeing that chief, said, This form and this gait cannot lie, and nothing but truth can proceed from them'" (KSA, XIV, 279), B. Atkinson (ed.), 'Essays: Second Series: Character', *The Complete Essays and Other Writings of Ralph Waldo Emerson* (New York: The Modern Library, 1950), 376; see also H. Weichelt, *Zarathustra-Kommentar* (Leipzig: Meiner, 1922), 222–7 and 291–4.

16 'The body is a great reason, a multiplicity with one sense, a war and a peace, one herd and one shepherd. Your small reason, what you call "spirit" is also a tool of your body, my brother, a small work – and plaything of your great reason' (KSA, IV, 39), F. Nietzsche, 'Of the Despisers of the Body', *Thus Spoke Zarathustra*.

17 Zarathustra is not a seducer, if he seduces it is because of the gift itself; he asks nothing for himself, and indeed asks to be forgotten and overcome as Nietzsche himself warns at the end of the prologue of *Ecce Homo*, echoing a passage from *Zarathustra*: 'You say you believe in Zarathustra? But what matters Zarathustra! You are my believers, but what matter all believers! You had not yet sought yourselves, then you found me. All believers do this; that's why all faith amounts to so little. Now I bid you lose me and find yourselves; and only when you have all denied me will I return to you. Indeed, with different eyes, my brothers, will I then seek my lost ones; with a different love will I love you then' (KSA, IV, 101–2), F. Nietzsche, 'On the Bestowing Virtue', *Thus Spoke Zarathustra*. Here Nietzsche puts forward an answer and an integration to Mt. 10.33: 'But whoever disowns me before others, I will disown before my Father in heaven'; on the 'difference' between Jesus and Zarathustra as regards the 'story' they announce, see K. Schlechta, *Nietzsches grosser Mittag* (Frankfurt am Main: Klostermann, 1954), 54 ff.

18 F. Nietzsche, 'Prologue', *Thus Spoke Zarathustra*.

19 In the sources from which Nietzsche obtains his information on the gift, the theme of the fatal gift is very recurrent. The term *gift* means both 'gift' and 'poison' in both the Anglo-Saxon and German language. The word comes, following the etymological path suggested by Émile Benveniste in his *Vocabulary of Indo-European Concepts and Society* dated 1971, by semantic loan from the Greek *dósis*, 'the act of offering', 'the promise to offer', which in a medical meaning valid both in Greek and Latin indicated a 'dose', and was gradually used as a substitute for *uenenum*, 'poison'. The wisdom of Zarathustra is poisonous in the sense that if it penetrates, it annihilates those who receive it, it turns them into other. '[A] staff upon whose golden knob a snake encircled the sun', this is what his disciples offer Zarathustra in the chapter 'On the bestowing virtue' as a farewell. The snake in the

Nietzschean imagination indicates the poisonous knowledge that is offered as a gift, it encircles the golden sun – gold being a metal that always gives and a supreme symbol of giving.

20 Think of the 'challenge' launched by Zarathustra 'to all religions'.

21 F. Nietzsche, 'Prologue', *Thus Spoke Zarathustra*.

22 Ibid., 'The Night Song', *Thus Spoke Zarathustra*.

23 Ibid.

24 Ibid., 'On the Friend', *Thus Spoke Zarathustra*.

25 Ibid., 'On the Pitying', *Thus Spoke Zarathustra*.

26 Ibid., 'On the Higher Man', *Thus Spoke Zarathustra*.

27 See also Mt. 22.36-40; the Gospel passage is actually composed of two passages from the Pentateuch: Deut. 6.5 ('Love the Lord your God with all your heart and with all your soul and with all your strength') and Lev. 19.18 ('love your neighbour as yourself'); what constitutes the radicalization of the teaching is rather the extension of love of one's neighbour to love of all, including enemies (Mt. 5.43 ff and Lk. 6.27 ff); see A. Fabris, *I paradossi dell'amore* (Brescia: Morcelliana, 2000), 89–107.

28 '*Theós agape*, means that God reveals Himself as such, as the neighbour, loving His neighbour who is called *plesios*. And it is the *philos* of those who, in turn, seek it, approximate it, become it themselves in seeking it. But the neighbour is always also other, the restless and striking *plesios*. In the *Agape* the agonic character of the relationship is not annulled at all, but precisely this is "saved": the dead separateness becomes recognition, distinction, compassion. The neighbour does not eliminate the stranger, the *hospes* does not erase the *thauma* of the appearance of the other. But heart and mind conform to their figures. Thus the God, for Hölderlin, conforms to the stranger, precisely by revealing himself as his neighbour – and *proximus* in himself, for in Life itself he keeps his flagellated Son within himself. *Theós agape* and *Theós xenos* cannot be separated', M. Cacciari, *Drammatica della prossimità*, 105.

29 'God personally immolating himself for the debt of man, God paying himself personally out of a pound of his own flesh, God as the one being who can deliver man from what man had become unable to deliver himself—the creditor playing scapegoat for his debtor, from love (can you believe it?), from love of his debtor!' (KSA, V, 331), F. Nietzsche, '"Guilt", "Bad Conscience" and the Like', *The Genealogy of Morals*, § 21.

30 M. Cacciari, *Drammatica della prossimità*, 95.

31 Ibid., 128.

32 *Supra*, FN 28.

33 F. Nietzsche, 'On Love of the Neighbour', *Thus Spoke Zarathustra*.

34 'Great indebtedness does not make people thankful, but vengeful instead; and if the small kindness is not forgotten then it will become a gnawing worm. "Be cold

in accepting! Let your accepting serve to distinguish!" – Thus I counsel those who have nothing to give away' (KSA, IV, 114), F. Nietzsche, 'On the Pitying', *Thus Spoke Zarathustra*.

35 R. W. Emerson, *Essays*, ed. by B. Atkinson (New York: The Modern Library, 1950), 403.

36 F. Nietzsche, 'On Love of the Neighbour', *Thus Spoke Zarathustra*.

37 'In one's friend one should have one's best enemy. You should be closest to him in heart when you resist him. [. . .] For your friend you cannot groom yourself beautifully enough, for you should be his arrow and longing for the over-man' (KSA, IV, 71–2), Nietzsche, 'On the Friend'.

38 In the sense of the *Edelkeit* of Meister Eckhart, for whom the *nobleman* is 'this man [that] has in one sense nothing in common with anything, that is, he is not formed or likened to this or that, and knows nothing of "nothing," so that one only finds in him pure life, being, truth, and goodness', M. O'C Walshe (ed. and trans.), 'The Nobleman', *The Complete Mystical Works of Meister Eckhart* (Freiburg: The Crossroad Publishing Company, 2009), 561–2. Although Sloterdijk has correctly described this same nobility as 'a position towards the future', in his reading he does not at all grasp the capacity to empty oneself and to renounce oneself which is inherent in the use of the adjective and instead insists on the active-proactive trait which raises the nobleman to lord; see P. Sloterdijk, *Über die Verbesserung der guten Nachricht. Nietzsches fünftes 'Evangelium'* (Frankfurt am Main: Suhrkamp, 2001), 49.

39 What Nietzsche calls 'star friendship' in *The Gay Science*; see *infra*, FN 47, 150–1.

40 F. Nietzsche, 'The Convalescent', *Thus Spoke Zarathustra*.

41 Ibid., 'On Great Longing', *Thus Spoke Zarathustra*.

42 Ibid., 'On the Three Evils', *Thus Spoke Zarathustra*.

Chapter 4

1 *"All my thoughts always speak to me of Love, / Yet have between themselves such difference / That while one bids me bow with mind and sense, A second saith, / 'Go to: look thou above; / 'The third one, hoping, yields me joy enough; / And with the last come tears, / I scarce know whence: / All of them craving pity in sore suspense, / Trembling with fears that the heart knoweth of."* in Dante Alighieri, *The New Life*, trans. by Dante Gabriel Rossetti (Auckland: The Floating Press, Kindle Edition, 2014).

2 F. Nietzsche, 'The Honey Sacrifice', *Thus Spoke Zarathustra*.

3 'sic ego nunc, quoniam haec ratio plerumque videtur tristior esse quibus non est tractata, retroque volgus abhorret ab hac, volui tibi suaviloquenti carmine Pierio

rationem esponere nostram et quasi musaeo dulci contingere melle, si tibi forte animum tali ratione tenere versibus in nostris possem, dum perspicis omnem naturam rerum qua constet compta figura', Lucretius, *De rerum natura*, I, 943–7.

4   As Bataille effectively observes, 'Cults require a bloody wasting of men and animals in *sacrifice*. In the etymological sense of the word, sacrifice is nothing other than the production of *sacred* things. From the very first, it appears that sacred things are constituted by an operation of loss: in particular, the success of Christianity must be explained by the value of the theme of the Son of God's ignominious crucifixion, which carries human dread to a representation of loss and limitless degradation', G. Bataille, 'The Notion of Expenditure' *Visions of Excess: Selected Writings 1927-1939*, ed. and trans. by Allan Stoekl (Minneapolis: University of Minnesota Press, 1985), 119. See also G. Bataille, *On Nietzsche*, trans. by S. Kendall (New York: SUNY Press, 2016).

5   '[. . .] the human sea – toward it I now cast my golden fishing rod and say: open up, you human abyss!

        Open up and toss me your fishes and glittering crabs! With my best bait today I bait the oddest human fishes!' (*KSA*, IV, 297), Nietzsche, 'The Honey Sacrifice'.

6   'As Jesus was walking beside the Sea of Galilee, he saw two brothers, Simon called Peter and his brother Andrew. They were casting a net into the lake, for they were fishermen. "Come, follow me," Jesus said, "and I will send you out to fish for people"' (Mt. 4.18-19).

7   As has been said, the will to love is first and foremost the will to give meaning in a world without meaning.

8   'The Gospels only speak of *sacrifices* in order to reject them and deny them any validity. [. . .] There is nothing in the Gospels to suggest that the death of Jesus is a sacrifice. [. . .] Thanks to the sacrificial reading, it has been possible for what we call Christendom to exist for fifteen or twenty centuries, that is to say, a culture has existed that is based, like all cultures (at least up to a certain point) on the mythological forms engendered by the founding mechanism. [. . .] A conception of this kind can only succeed in concealing yet again the real meaning and function of the Passion: one of subverting sacrifice and barring it from working ever again by forcing the founding mechanism out into the open, writing it down in the text of all the Gospels [. . .] exposing to the light of the sun the victimization mechanism', R. Girard, 'A Non-Sacrificial Reading of the Gospel Text', in *Things Hidden Since the Foundation of the World* (London: A&C Black, 2003), 180–1.

9   'The very word "Christianity" is a misunderstanding;—in reality there has been only one Christian, and he died on the cross. The "Evangelium" *died* on the cross. What was called "Evangelium" from that hour onwards was already the antithesis of what *he* had lived: "*bad* tidings," a *Dysangelium*. It is false to the verge of absurdity, to see in a "belief" (perhaps in the belief of salvation through Christ) the

distinguishing mark of the Christian: Christian *practice* alone (a life such as he who died on the cross *lived*) is Christian' (*KSA*, VI, 211), Nietzsche, *Twilight of the Idols and The Anti-Christ*. From this point of view one can read Dionysus's opposition to the Crucifix: 'Dionysus *versus* "Christ"; here you have the contrast. It is *not* a difference in regard to the martyrdom, – but the latter has a different meaning. Life itself – Life's eternal fruitfulness and recurrence caused anguish, destruction, and the will to annihilation. In the other case, the suffering of the "Christ as the Innocent One" stands as an objection against Life, it is the formula of Life's condemnation. [. . .] God on the Cross is a curse upon Life, a signpost directing people to deliver themselves from it; – Dionysus cut into pieces is a *promise* of Life: it will be for ever born anew, and rise afresh from destruction', F. Nietzsche, *The Will To Power*, trans. by Anthony M. Ludovici (Delhi Open Books, Kindle Edition, n.d.), § 1052.

10 'In itself, Jesus could not wish aught by his death but to give publicly the strongest test, the *demonstration* of his doctrine. . . . But his disciples were far from *forgiving* this death – which would have been evangelical in the highest sense [. . .] Just the most unevangelical of feelings, *revenge*, again came to the fore' (*KSA*, VI, 142), Nietzsche, *Twilight of the Idols and The Anti-Christ*, § 40.

11 É. Benveniste, *Le Vocabulaire des institutions indo-européennes*, 92; more generally on the theme of hospitality, pp. 87–101.

12 In the wake of Marcel Mauss, Benveniste states that 'hospitality is clarified by the reference to the *potlatch* of which it is an attenuated form. It is based on the idea that one man is bound to another (*hostis* always has a reciprocal value) by the obligation to compensate for a certain service he has received', É. Benveniste, *Le Vocabulaire des institutions indo-européennes*, 92.

13 'Indeed, there sitting all together were the ones he had passed by during the day: the king on the right and king on the left, the old magician, the pope, the voluntary beggar, the shadow, the conscientious of spirit, the sad soothsayer and the ass; the ugliest human being, however, had donned a crown and draped two purple sashes around himself – for like all ugly people he loved to disguise himself and act beautiful. But in the midst of this gloomy company stood Zarathustra's eagle, bristling and restless because he was pressed to answer too much for which his pride had no answer; meanwhile the wise snake hung around his neck.' (*KSA*, IV, 346–7), F. Nietzsche, 'The Welcome', *Thus Spoke Zarathustra*.

14 Nietzsche, 'The Welcome', *Thus Spoke Zarathustra*.

15 Ibid.

16 F. Nietzsche, 'The Ass Festival', *Thus Spoke Zarathustra*.

17 '"To my last sin?" cried Zarathustra, and laughed scornfully at his own words. [. . .] "Pity! Pity for the higher men!" he cried, and his face transformed to bronze. "Well then! That – has its time! My suffering and my pity – what do they matter! Do I

strive for happiness? I strive for my work!'" (*KSA*, IV, 408), F. Nietzsche, 'The Sign', *Thus Spoke Zarathustra*.

18   F. Nietzsche, 'The Welcome', *Thus Spoke Zarathustra*.

19   'Meanwhile, however, the higher men in Zarathustra's cave had awakened and were forming a procession, in order to approach Zarathustra and offer their morning greeting [. . .] But as they reached the door of the cave, and the noise of their footsteps preceded them, the lion started violently, turned suddenly away from Zarathustra and leaped, roaring wildly, toward the cave; and the higher men, when they heard it roaring, all cried out as if with one voice, and fled back and disappeared in a flash [. . .] Well then! The lion came, my children are near, Zarathustra became ripe, my hour came', (*KSA*, IV, 407–8), Nietzsche, 'The Sign', *Thus Spoke Zarathustra*.

20   'Well then! They're sleeping still, these higher men, while I am awake: they are not my proper companions! [. . .] they do not understand what the signs of my morning are, my step – is not a wake up call for them', (*KSA*, IV, 405), Nietzsche, 'The Sign', *Thus Spoke Zarathustra*.

21   Nietzsche, 'The Welcome', *Thus Spoke Zarathustra*.

22   In this sense, one understands what freedom the will leads to for Nietzsche in a clear echo of his youthful writings influenced by Emerson, which, however, does not allow for any surrender to the extinction of the will in Schopenhauer's *noluntas*: 'Willing liberates: that is the true teaching of will and liberty – thus Zarathustra teaches it. No more willing and no more esteeming and no more creating! Oh, if only this great weariness would always keep away from me! Even in knowing I feel only my will's lust to beget and to become; and if there is innocence in my knowledge, then this happens because the will to beget is in it' (*KSA*, IV, 111), F. Nietzsche, 'On the Blessed Isles', *Thus Spoke Zarathustra*.

23   *Supra*, FN 38, 121.

24   F. Nietzsche, 'On Free Death', *Thus Spoke Zarathustra*.

25   Ibid.; the 'nobility' of Jesus is to be read in parallel with the definition of 'idiot', in the Dostoevsky sense, an expression with which Nietzsche describes ('with the rigor of the physiologist') the psychological profile of Jesus in *The Antichrist*, alluding to his simplicity and innocence, typical of the perfect poor. A reference that prevents one from reading the 'nobility' of Jesus as the distinctive trait and consequence of his 'genius' or his 'heroicity' demanded by Renan's reading, against which Nietzsche rails (see *KSA*, VI, 199–200; *The Antichrist*, § 29).

26   Which is an ethical action but in the sense of the 'supreme action' into which the Dionysian is translated in *Zarathustra*.

27   Zarathustra is in fact a messenger and bearer of a gift that he has in turn received from the depths of his soul.

28   Nietzsche, *The Gay Science*, § 109.

29 'I say to you: one must still have chaos in oneself in order to give birth to a dancing star. I say to you: you still have chaos in you' (*KSA*, IV, 19), Nietzsche, 'Prologue', *Thus Spoke Zarathustra*. On the notion of Chaos in Nietzsche, allow me to refer to my *Volontà d'amore*, in particular pp. 102 ff. 'Friendship is the hidden "bond" of love (φιλὶα, *filìa*) in which man, who opens himself to the idea of the *Übermensch*, can see Χάος (*Chaos*) which, like a common essence, like a super soul (*Überseele*), constitutes the immediacy in which every authentic relationship with the All is possible' (ibid., 144).

30 M. Eckhart, 'The Talks of Instruction', *The Complete Mystical Works of Meister Eckhart*, translated and edited by M. O'C. Walshe (The Crossroad Publishing Company, 2009), 488.

31 Unlike the other Gospels (Mk 8.35; Mt. 10.39; Lk. 17.33), John's Gospel speaks explicitly of *zoé*, that is, of 'being alive', 'life in the full sense', as opposed to *psyché* as a simple 'being-in-life': 'anyone who loves their life [*psyché*] will lose it, while anyone who hates their life [*psyché*] in this world will keep it for eternal [*zoé*] life' (Jn 12.24-25); see Jullien, *Ressources du christianisme*, 57.

32 M. Vannini, *Introduzione a Eckhart. Profilo e testi* (Florence: Le Lettere, 2014), 34.

33 M. Eckhart, 'The Nobleman', 561.

34 As Vannini observes, Eckhart believes that with the love that leads to 'detachment' man is somehow able to open himself to grace: 'Almost due to a physical law, whereby every void must be filled, he who makes the void in and of himself is filled by the divine being. It is a necessary law, which does not depend on God's will: God has to do it, he cannot help it', M. Vannini, *Introduzione a Eckhart*, 30.

35 'The *sixth* stage is when a man is de-formed and transformed by God's eternity, and has attained total forgetfulness of transitory, temporal life and is drawn and translated into a divine image, having become the child of God', M. Eckhart, 'The Nobleman', 559.

36 Nietzsche, 'Prologue'.

37 Authorizing, for example, the reading of Bataille.

38 Nietzsche, 'On the Blessed Isles', *Thus Spoke Zarathustra*.

39 Ibid., 'The Other Dance Song', *Thus Spoke Zarathustra*.

40 F. Jullien, *Ressources du christianisme*, 65.

41 According to that 'de-deification' of nature and the subsequent 'naturalization' of man of which we read in § 109 of *The Gay Science*: 'But when shall we ever be done with our caution and care? When will all these shadows of God cease to darken our minds? When will we complete our de-deification [*entgöttlicht*] of nature? When may we begin to "naturalize" [*vernatürlichen*] humanity in terms of a pure, newly discovered, newly redeemed nature?' (*KSA*, III, 468–9), Nietzsche, *The Gay Science*, §109.

42 'Now man recognizes Nature, and rediscovers in himself a new love: that same *Chaos des Alls* that animates himself and Nature as a whole. A first step is taken, but it is not enough. In order for the *naturalization* of man to be said to be accomplished in the transvaluation of every value, a "new" *humanization* of Nature must also be realized: and this basically means the infinite aspiration to the *Übermensch*, as a new meaning to be assigned to the earth, or rather as an "active engine" of an overwhelming dynamics that only the love that infinitely gives is able to symbolically represent, in contrast to the figure (*Typus*) of the *last man*, the a-typical of the *Over-man*', Corriero, *Volontà d'amore,* 145; on the new humanization of nature see also pp. 145–50.

43 As Jullien comments on John's Gospel: 'Christ is the one who, within Being, opens the door to the happening of the Event. As if to say that from the beginning John replaces the ontological statute, which among the Greeks condemned becoming in the name of Being and made it incapable of an advent, with another possible statute, a Christic statute, such as to anchor the becoming within Being and to make it able to reform [. . .]. Pushing to the extreme the thought of becoming-advent, John essentially tells us two things. On the one hand, that the event can change everything: that we can "become healthy", because we were sick, that it can make us enter a totally different life and that, through this, the impossible becomes possible. On the other, that when the event has reached its decisive point, in most cases we do not perceive it from the outside: "among you stands one [Christ] you do not know"' (Jn 1.26), F. Jullien, *Ressources du christianisme*, 45–50.

44 Martin Heidegger's reflection on *Ereignis* moves in this direction, particularly in the 1962 conference *Time and Being*, in which he clarifies how Western thought privileged the gift of being – being because it is present – that is, the *Gabe*, what is given in the *Es gibt*, leaving aside instead the *Es* of the *Es gibt* which remains indeterminable in terms of ontotheology; on this subject, please refer to my *The Absolute and the Event. Schelling after Heidegger*, trans. by Vanessa Di Stefano (London-New York: Bloomsbury, 2020).

45 According to what is also stated in Rom. 1.16–8.39.

46 In the sense of Schelling's positive philosophy, which has as its object mythology and revelation, that is the process of creation and recreation. On this subject, see my 'Pensare la natura. La Naturphilosophie di Schelling alla luce della sua filosofia positiva' in *Annuario filosofico*, 30, 2014, pp. 171–93.

47 The passage from *The Gay Science* sums up well the Nietzschean sense of friendship that we described earlier and this particular relationship between solitary people; see *KSA*, III, 523–4, F. Nietzsche, *The Gay Science*, § 279, on this point see the previously mentioned M. Cacciari, *L'arcipelago*, 143–54.

48 'There, where the state ends – look there, my brothers! Do you not see it, the rainbow and the bridges of the overman? –' (*KSA*, IV, 64), F. Nietzsche, 'On the

New Idol', *Thus Spoke Zarathustra*. I have shown elsewhere how the State form will, if anything, be understood as functional to the overcoming in the fragments destined for *The Will to Power*: 'At most the State can perform the *contractual*, oppositional function, which allows the overcoming and transvaluation of all values. If the State loses its "vocation", obliterating itself under the metaphysical veiling, then it tends to perpetuate itself in its own decay and corruption; vice versa, if it recovers its "necessary", yet transitory, limiting function, it allows the *free* evolution of the *Überwindung*', Corriero, *Vertigini della ragione*, 146.

49 F. Nietzsche, *Twilight of the Idols* and *The Antichrist*, § 29.

50 Ibid., § 43.

Afterword

1 'There, where the state ends – look there, my brothers! Do you not see it, the rainbow and the bridges of the overman?' F. Nietzsche, 'On the New Idol', *Thus spoke Zarathustra*.

2 F. Nietzsche, *Human, All Too Human, I* (New York: The Big Nest, Kindle Edition, 2015), *376* (my italics).

3 See F. Nietzsche, *Beyond Good and Evil*.

4 Nietzsche, *The Gay Science*, § 279.

5 Contrary to the Nietzschean meaning of friendship: 'Fellow rejoicing [*Mitfreude*], not fellow suffering [*Mitleiden*], makes the friend' (F. Nietzsche, *Human, All Too Human*, I, 499).

6 The use of the expression 'terrestrial' by Nietzsche to define enmity is certainly significant, particularly if we think of Carl Schmitt's subsequent reflections on the Political and the enemy, and the link he recognizes between law and earth; see in particular C. Schmitt, *Land und Meer: eine weltgeschichtliche Betrachtung* (Leipzig: Reclam, 1942); ibid., *Nomos der Erde im Völkerrecht des Jus Publicum Europaeum* (Köln: Greven, 1950).

Bibliography

Abel, G. *Nietzsche. Die Dynamik der Willen zur Macht*. Berlin and New York: Walter de Gruyter, 1998.

Agamben, G. *Potentialities. Collected Essays in Philosophy*. Stanford, CA: Stanford University Press, 1999.

Aime, M. 'Da Mauss al MAUSS', the introduction to the Italian ed. of M. Mauss, *Saggio sul dono* (*The Gift*). Torino: Einaudi, 2002.

Alderman, H. *Nietzsche's Gift*. Athens, OH: Ohio University Press, 1979.

Allison, D. B. (ed). *The New Nietzsche. Contemporary Style of Interpretation*. New York: MIT Press, 1977.

Aristotle. *The Complete Works of Aristotle: The Revised Oxford Translation*, ed. J. Barnes. 2 vols. Princeton: Princeton University Press, 1971.

Bataille, G. 'The Notion of Expenditure' in *Visions of Excess: Selected Writings 1927–1939*, ed. and trans. by Allan Stoekl. Minneapolis: University of Minnesota Press, 1985.

Bataille, G. *On Nietzsche*, trans. by S. Kendall. New York: SUNY Press, 2016.

Benveniste, É. *Le Vocabulaire des institutions indo-européennes*, 2 vols. Paris: Minuit, 1969.

Bianchi, E. and Cacciari, M. *Ama il prossimo tuo*. Bologna: il Mulino, 2011.

Bianchi, E. *Dono e Perdono*. Torino: Einaudi, 2014.

Bodei, R. *La vita delle cose*. Roma-Bari: Laterza, 2014.

Brobjer, T. H. *Nietzsche's Philosophical Context: An Intellectual Biography*. Urbana and Chicago: University of Illinois, 2008.

Cacciari, M. 'Sul Presupposto. Schelling e Rosenweig', *Aut aut*, 210–11 (1986): 43–65.

Cacciari, M. *Dell'Inizio*. Milano: Adelphi, 1990.

Cacciari, M. *L'arcipelago*. Milano: Adelphi, 1997.

Cacciari, M. 'Il Gesù di Nietzsche', *Micromega*, 5 (2000): 193–202.

Cacciari, M. *Della cosa ultima*. Milano: Adelphi, 2004.

Caillé, A. *Antropologie du don: Le tiers paradigme*. Paris: Desclée de Brouwer, 2000.

Clark, M. *Nietzsche on Truth and Philosophy*. Cambridge: Cambridge University Press, 1990.

Colli, G. *Dopo Nietzsche*. Milano: Adelphi, 1974.

Colli, G. *Scritti su Nietzsche*. Milano: Adelphi, 1980

Corriero, E. C. 'Schelling e Nietzsche. Un percorso teoretico', *Annuario filosofico*, 28 (2012): 450–73.

Corriero, E. C. *Nietzsche's Death of God and Italian Philosophy*. London and New York: Rowman & Littlefield, 2016.

Corriero, E. C. *Vertigini della ragione. Schelling e Nietzsche*. Preface by M. Cacciari. Torino: Rosenberg & Sellier, 2018.

Corriero, E. C. and Vercellone, F. (eds). *Cristalli di Storicità. Saggi in onore di Remo Bodei*. Torino: Rosenberg & Sellier, 2019.

Corriero, E. C. *The Absolute and the Event. Schelling after Heidegger*. London and New York: Bloomsbury, 2020.

Cousineau, R. H. *Zarathustra and the Ethical Ideal. Timely Meditations on Philosophy*. Amsterdam: Benjamins Publishing, 1991.

Dante, *The New Life*, trans. by Dante Gabriel Rossetti. Aukland: The Floating Press, Kindle Edition, 2014.

Danto, A. *Nietzsche as Philosopher*. New York: Columbia University Press, new edition 2005.

Deleuze, G. *Nietzsche et la philosophie*. Paris: PUF, 1962.

Derrida, J. *Éperons: les styles de Nietzsche*. Paris: Flammarion, 1978. Translated by B. Harlow as *Spurs: Nietzsche's Styles/Éperons: les styles de Nietzsche*. Chicago: University of Chicago Press, 1981.

Derrida, J. *Posizions*. Paris: Les Edition de Minuit, 1972. Translated by A. Bass as *Positions*. Chicago: University of Chicago Press, 1981.

Derrida, J. *Donner le temps. La fausse monnaie*. Paris: Galilée, 1991.

Derrida, J. *Donner la mort*. Paris: Galilée, 1999.

Dickinson, E. *Bolts of Melody. New Poems of Emily Dickinson*, eds Mabel Loomis Todd and Millicent Todd Bingham. New York: Harper, 1945.

Eckhart, M. 'The Nobleman', *The Complete Mystical Works of*, ed. and trans. by M. O'C Walshe. Freiburg: The Crossroad Publishing Company, 2009.

Emerson, R. W. *The Complete Essays and Other Writings of Ralph Waldo Emerson*. New York: The Modern Library, 1950.

Emerson, R. W. *The Collected Works of Ralph Waldo Emerson*. Cambridge: Harvard University Press, 1950.

Esposito, R. *Communitas. Origine e destino della comunità*. Torino: Einaudi, new edition 2006.

Esposito, R. *Immunitas. Protezione e negazione della vita*. Torino: Einaudi, new edition 2020.

Fabris, A. *I paradossi dell'amore*. Brescia: Morcelliana, 2000.

Fabris, A. *TeorEtica. Filosofia della relazione*. Brescia: Morcelliana, 2010.

Fabris, A. *Relazione: una filosofia performativa*. Brescia: Morcelliana, 2016.

Ferraris, M. *Nietzsche e la filosofia del novecento*, 2nd edn. Milan: Bompiani, 2009.

Figal, G. *Nietzsche – eine philosophische Einführung*. Stuttgart: Reclam, 1999.

Fornari, G. *Da Dioniso a Cristo: conoscenza e sacrificio nel mondo greco e nella civiltà occidentale*. Torino: Marietti 1820, 2006.

Gadamer, H.-G. 'Das Drama Zarathustras', *Nietzsches-Studien*, 15 (1986): 1–15.

Gebhard, W. *Nietzsches Totalismus: Philosophie der Natur zwischen Verklärung und Verhängnis*. Berlin and New York: Walter de Gruyter, 1983.

Gerhardt, V. *Vom Willen zur Macht. Anthropologie und Metaphysik der Macht am exemplarischen Fall Nietzsches*. München: Beck Verlag, 1996.

Gerhardt, V. *Also sprach Zarathustra. Klassiker Auslegen*. Berlin: Akademie Verlag, 2012.

Giametta, S. *Commento allo 'Zarathustra'*. Milano: Bruno Mondadori, 1996.

Girard, R. 'A Non-Sacrificial Reading of the Gospel Text', in *Things Hidden Since the Foundation of the World*. London: A&C Black, 2003.

Godbout, J. T. *L'esprit du don*. Montréal and Paris: Éditions La Découverte, 1992.

Heidegger, M. *Nietzsche*. 2 vol. Pfullingen: Neske, 1961.

Heidegger, M. *On Time and Being*, eds J. Macquarrie and E. Robinson. Oxford: Blackwell, 1962.

Higgins, K. M. *Nietzsche's Zarathustra*. Philadelphia: Tample University Press, 1987.

Honneth, A. *Kampf um Anerkennung – Zur moralischen Grammatik sozialer Konflikte*. Frankfurt am Main: Suhrkamp, 1994.

Honneth, A. *Das Ich im Wir: Studien in Anerkennungstheorie*. Frankfurt am Main: Suhrkamp, 2010.

Honneth, A. *Anerkennung. Eine europäische Ideengeschichte*. Frankfurt am Main: Suhrkamp, 2018.

Hunt, L. H. *Nietzsche and the Origin of Virtue*. London: Routledge, 1991.

Jaspers, K. *Nietzsche, Einführung in das Verständnis seines Philosophierens*. Berlin: de Gruyter, 1936.

Janz, C. P. *Friedrich Nietzsche. Biographie in drei Bände*. München/Wien: Hanser, 1978–1979.

Jullien, F. *Ressources du christianisme: Mais sans y entrer par la foi*. Paris: L'Herne, 2018.

Jung, C. G. *Nietzsche's Zarathustra. Notes of the Seminar Given in 1934–1939 by C.G. Jung*, ed. by J. L. Jarret, 2 vol. Princeton: Routledge, 1988.

Kaufmann, W. *Nietzsche. Philosopher, Psicolofigist, Antichrist*. Princeton: Princeton University Press, 1975.

Klossowski, P. *Nietzsche et le circle vicieux*. Paris: Mercure de France, 1969.

Lampert, L. *Nietzsche's Teaching: An Interpretation of 'Thus Spoke Zarathustra'*. New Haven: Yale University Press, 1986.

Lévi-Strauss, C. 'Introduction à l'œuvre de Mauss', in M. Mauss, *Sociologie et Anthropologie*. Paris: PUF, 1950.

Lewis, C. S. *Mere Christianity*. Oxford: Pte. Ltd., 1952.

Löwith, K. *Nietzsches Philosophie der ewigen Wiederkehr des Gleichen*. Stuttgart: Kohlhammer, 1935.

Löwith, K. *Von Hegel zu Nietzsche. Der revolutionäre Bruch im Denken des neunzehnten Jahrhunderts*. Stuttgart: Metzler, 1954.

Lukács, G. *Die Zerstörung der Vernunft. Der Weg des Irrationalismus von Schelling zu Hitler*. Berlin: Aufbau-Verlag, 1954.

Marion, J.-L. *Réduction et donation. Recherches sur Husserl, Heidegger et la phénoménologie*. Paris: PUF, 1989.

Marion, J.-L. *Etant donné. Essai d'une phénoménologie de la donation*. Paris: PUF, 1997.

Marion, J.-L. *Dialogo con l'amore*, ed. by U. Perone. Torino: Rosenberg & Sellier, 2007.

Masini, F. *Lo scriba del caos. Interpretazione di Nietzsche.* Bologna: il Mulino, 1978; second edn, ed. by E. C. Corriero. Torino: Nino Aragno Editore, 2019.

Mauss, M. *Sociologie et Anthropologie.* Paris: PUF, 1950.

Mauss, M. *Œuvres.* Paris: Minuit, 1968–9.

Mauss, M. *The Gift. The Form and Reason for Exchange in Archaic Societies,* trans. by W. D. Halls. London: Routledge, 1990.

Messer, A. *Erläuterungen zu Nietzsches 'Zarathustra'.* Stuttgart: Strecker & Schröder, 1922.

Moiso, F. *Nietzsche e le scienze.* Milan: CUEM, 1999; second edn, ed. by Matteo D'Alfonso. Torino: Rosenberg & Sellier, 2020.

Montinari, M. *Che cosa ha detto Nietzsche,* 2nd edn. Milan: Adelphi, 1999.

Müller-Lauter, W. *Nietzsche. Seine Philosophie der Gegensätze und die Gegensätze seiner Philosophie.* Berlin and New York: de Gruyter, 1971.

Müller-Lauter, W. *Über Freiheit und Chaos in Nietzsche-Intrpretationen,* 3 vol. vol. II. Berlin: de Gruyter, 1999.

Nietzsche, F. Sämtliche Werke. *Kritische Studienausgabe,* eds G. Colli and M. Montinari, 15 vol. Berlin and New York: Walter de Gruyter, 1967–77, e1988 [KSA].

Nietzsche, F. *Sämtliche Briefe, Kritische Studienausgabe,* eds G. Colli and M. Montinari, 6 vol. Berlin and New York: Walter de Gruyter, 1986.

Nietzsche, F. *Ecce Homo.* Waxkeep Publishing, Kindle Edition, n.d.

Nietzsche, F. *The Will to Power,* trans. by Anthony M. Ludovici. Delhi Open Books, Kindle Edition, n.d.

Nietzsche, F. 'Beyond Good and Evil', trans. by Helen Zimmern, in *The Complete Works of Friedrich Nietzsche.* Edinburgh and London: T. N. Foulis, 1909.

Nietzsche, F. *The Gay Science,* trans. by Walter Kaufmann. New York: Knopf Doubleday Publishing Group – Vintage Books, Kindle Edition, 1974.

Nietzsche, F. '"Guilt", "Bad Conscience and the Like"' in *The Genealogy of Morals.* New York: Dover Thrift Editions, Dover Publications, Kindle Edition, 2003.

Nietzsche, F. *Thus Spoke Zarathustra,* ed. by Robert Pippin and trans. by Adrian Del Caro. Cambridge: Cambridge University Press, 2006.

Nietzsche, F. *Ecce Homo.* Oxford: OUP Oxford World's Classics, Kindle Edition, 2007.

Nietzsche, F. *Human, All Too Human.* New York: The Big Nest, Kindle Edition, 2015.

Nietzsche, F. *Twilight of the Idols and The Anti-Christ,* trans. by Thomas Common. Kansas: Digireads.com Publishing, Kindle Edition, 2018.

Norman, J. and Welchman, A. (eds). *The New Schelling.* New York: Continuum, 2004.

Naumann, G. *Zarathustra Commentar.* Leipzig: Verlag von Haessel, 1899–1901.

Pasqualotto, G. *Saggi su Nietzsche.* Milano: Franco Angeli, 1988.

Pasqualotto, G. *Commento Published Together with the Italian Edition of Nietzsche, Così parlò Zarathustra,* trans. by Sossio Giametta. Milano: Rizzoli, 1988.

Penzo, G. *Il superamento di Zarathustra: Nietzsche e il nazionalsocialismo.* Rome: Armando, 1987.

Pieper, A. *Ein Seil geknüpft zwischen Tier und Übermensch. Philosophisches Erläuterungen zu Nietzsches erstem 'Zarathustra'.* Stuttgart: Klett-Cotta, 1990;

Pippin, R. P. *Nietzsche, Psychology and First Philosophy*. Chicago: University of Chicago Press, 2010.

Riehl, A. *Friedrich Nietzsche, der Künstler und der Denker*. Stuttgart: Frommann, 1901.

Rorty, R. and G. Vattimo. *Il futuro della religione. Solidarietà, carità, ironia*, ed. by S. Zabala, Milano: Garzanti, 2005. Translated by W. McCuaig as *The Future of Religion*. New York: Columbia University Press, 2005.

Rosen, S. *The Mask of Enlightenment: Nietzsche's 'Zarathustra'*. Cambridge: Cambridge University Press, 1995.

Salomé, L. *Nietzsche*, trans. by Siegfried Mandel. Urbana and Chicago: University of Illinois Press, 2001.

Schlechta, K. *Nietzsches grosser Mittag*. Frankfurt am Main: Klostermann, 1953.

Schmitt, C. *Land und Meer: eine weltgeschichtliche Betrachtung*. Leipzig: Reclam, 1942.

Schmitt, C. *Nomos der Erde im Völkerrecht des Jus Publicum Europaeum*. Köln: Greven, 1950.

Schmitt, C. *The Tirrany of Values and Other Texts*, ed. by Russell A. Berman and Samuel Garrett Zeitlin. Candor, NY: Telos Press, 2018.

Seneca, Lucio Anneo. *On Benefits*. Trans. M. Griffin, and B. Inwood. Chicago: Chicago University Press, 2011.

Severino, E. *La struttura originaria*. Brescia: La Scuola, 1958.

Severino, E. *Destino della necessità*. Milano: Adelphi, 1980.

Severino, E. *L'anello del ritorno*. Milano: Adelphi, 1999.

Shapiro, G. *Alcyone: Nietzsche on Gift, Noise, and Women*. Albany: SUNY, 1991.

Siegel, G. *Nietzsches Zarathustra: Gehalt und Gestalt*. Münich: Reinhardt, 1938.

Sloterdijk, P. *Der Denker auf der Bühne. Nietzsches Materialismus*. Frankfurt am Main: Suhrkamp, 1986.

Sloterdijk, P. *Über die Verbesserung der guten Nachricht. Nietzsches fünftes 'Evangelium'*. Frankfurt am Main: Suhrkamp, 2001.

Starobinski, J. 'Don fastueux et don pervers', *Annales E.S.C.*, 41 (1986): 7–26.

Tagliapietra, A. *Il dono del filosofo. Sul gesto originario della filosofia*. Torino: Einaudi, 2009.

Vannini, M. *Introduzione a Eckhart. Profilo e testi*. Firenze: Le Lettere, 2014.

Vattimo, G. *Il soggetto e la maschera*. Milano: Bompiani, 1974.

Vattimo, G. *La fine della modernità*. Milano: Garzanti, 1991.

Vattimo, G. *Dialogo con Nietzsche*. Milano: Garzanti, 2000.

Vattimo, G. *Introduzione a Heidegger*. Roma and Bari: Laterza, 2001.

Vattimo, G. *Della realtà*. Milano: Garzanti, 2012.

Verker, W. *Nietzsche and Friendship*. London and New York: Bloomsbury, 2019.

Vidal, D. 'Les trois Grâces ou l'allégorie du Don', *Gradhiva*, 9 (1991): 13–47.

Weichelt, H. *Friedrich Nietzsche: Also sprach Zarathustra, Erklärt und gewürdig*. Leipzig: Duerr, 1910; second edition revised as *Zarathustra-Kommentar*. Leipzig: Meiner, 1922.

Index

force   5, 6, 7, 8, 9, 10, 14, 22, 30, 38, 40,
     54, 56, 58, 61, 63, 105, notes 113
Fornari, Giuseppe   notes 111
freedom   12, 15, 16, 17, 30, 47, 57, 70, 76,
     101, 102, notes 108, 114, 122
friend   3, 13, 24, 54, 63, 69–77, 80, 83–90,
     92, 93, 96, 99–106, notes 113, 114,
     115, 118
   enemy   1, 24, 49, 54, 73–5, 83, 84, 86,
     102–6, notes 108, 113, 118
   friendship   13, 54, 69, 70, 73, 74, 75,
     86, 89, 96, 99–106, notes 119, 122,
     124, 125
   philia   13, 72, 74, 100, 101
   star friendship   96, 99, 105, 106, notes
     119

Gegebenheit   3
Gerhardt, Volker   notes 107
Geworfenheit   3
Giametta, Sossio   notes 107, 111
gift
   beneficium   11, 13–15
   gift of grace   12, 90
   gift of love   12, 19, 36, 39, 66, 76, 92, 93
   gift of wisdom   2, 27, 37, 51, 54, 59,
     63, 64, 76, 90, 93, notes 113
   munus   11, 13–15, 21, 22
Girard, René   82, notes 111, 120
God   2, 3, 11, 12, 15, 17, 23, 32–4, 35, 37,
     38–48, 56–60, 62, 65, 66, 71, 72, 80,
     82, 83, 85, 88, 90–3, 95, 104, 105,
     notes 108–12, 114, 115, 118, 119,
     120, 123
   death of God   2, 3, 23, 37, 38, 39, 40,
     43, 45, 46, 57–60, 66, 80, 82, 85, 88,
     92, 93, 104, notes 114, 115
Godbout, Jacques T.   17, notes 108, 109
Gospel   1, 2, 27, 34, 36, 48, 55, 60, 66,
     70, 72, 77, 81, 94, 95, notes 110–14,
     118, 120, 122, 123
   Fifth Gospel   1, 27, 36, 48, 55, 66, 70,
     notes 110
grace   12, 15, 18, 19, 22, 30, 35, 36, 90,
     92, notes 108, 109, 112, 113, 123
   gratia   36
   gratuitousness   12, 13, 17, 20, 30, 36,
     44, 60, notes 109, 113
grounding   89, 90, 92, 95

hau   6
Heidegger, Martin   notes 109, 116, 124
Heraclitus   notes 112
Hölderlin, Friedrich   notes 118
Honneth, Axel   notes 108
honour   10
hospitality   24, 42, 79, 80, 83, 84, notes
     109, 121
   guest   3, 24, 63, 83, 84, 86
   hospes   24, 83, notes 118
   hostis   24, 83, notes 109, 121

indifference   8, 9, 48, 58
intention   5–7, 14, 21, 22, 29, 36, 40, 41,
     56, 70

Jaspers, Karl   notes 113
Jesus   1, 12, 33, 34, 35, 49, 81, 82, 89, 91,
     94, 97, notes 111, 113, 117, 120–2
Jullien, François   94, notes 116, 122–4

knowledge   2, 31, 32, 44, 45, 50, 54, 55,
     63, 64, 76, 83, notes 117, 122

Lévi-Strauss, Claude   6, notes 107
loneliness   41, 43, 67–9, 73–5, 80, 81, 99
love   1, 2, 12, 13, 15, 18, 19, 23–5, 27, 31,
     32, 34–7, 39, 41–52, 54–60, 62, 64,
     66–8, 70–7, 79–97, 103, 104, 106,
     notes 107, 108, 112, 113, 114, 115,
     116, 117, 118, 120, 121, 122, 123
   affirmative love   42, 45
   agape   15, 37, 41, 56, 71, 72, notes
     114, 118
   christian love   15, 23, 42, 103, 104,
     106, notes 108, 114
   compassionate love   2, 43, 70, 72, 82,
     83, 85, 86, 104, 106, notes 114
   law of love   12, 36, 37, 48, 68, 96
   new love   2, 45, 49, 72, 79, 85, 87
Löwith, Karl   notes 108

man   12, 18, 28, 31, 32, 34, 35, 40–8, 50,
     52, 55, 57, 59, 61, 63, 66, 69, 72, 73,
     82, 89–91, 94–6, 99, 103, 104, notes
     115, 116, 118, 121, 122, 123
   higher men   24, 80
   höheren Menschen   24, 80
   last man   45, 59, notes 123